Accessing U.S. Government Information, Revised and Expanded Edition

Accessing U.S. Government Information, Revised and Expanded Edition

Subject Guide to Jurisdiction of the Executive and Legislative Branches

Compiled by **Jerrold Zwirn**

Bibliographies and Indexes in Law and
Political Science, Number 24

Greenwood Press
Westport, Connecticut • London

Library of Congress Cataloging-in-Publication Data

Zwirn, Jerrold.
   Accessing U.S. government information : subject guide to
jurisdiction of the executive and legislative branches / compiled by
Jerrold Zwirn.—Rev. and expanded ed.
      p.   cm.—(Bibliographies and indexes in law and political
science, ISSN 0742-6909 ; no. 24)
   Includes bibliographical references and index.
   ISBN 0-313-29765-7 (alk. paper)
      1. Government publications—United States—Indexes. 2. United
States. Congress—Directories. 3. Administrative agencies—United
States—Directories. 4. Executive departments—United States–
Directories. I. Title. II. Series.
   Z1223.Z7Z88   1996
   [J83]
   015.73′053—dc20   95-38638

British Library Cataloguing in Publication Data is available.

Library of Congress Catalog Card Number: 95-38638
ISBN: 0-313-29765-7
ISSN: 0742-6909

First published in 1996

Greenwood Press, 88 Post Road West, Westport, CT 06881
An imprint of Greenwood Publishing Group, Inc.

Printed in the United States of America

The paper used in this book complies with the
Permanent Paper Standard issued by the National
Information Standards Organization (Z39.48–1984).

10 9 8 7 6 5 4 3 2

To Larry — who ponders how history transforms ancient error
into modern dogma

To Maryellen — who knows the right recipes for more than
just desserts

Contents

viii Contents

Introduction

The need for this much revised new edition stems from the variable nature of national issues and the versatile array of public responses. The organic relationship between government and society demands that the former continually adapt to the latter. A federal agenda is never final but is always in progress, reflecting the impact of social and economic change, international events, and technological innovation. This affects the complexion of policy perspectives, public purposes, and political priorities.

Regular elections, enduring concerns, and urgent contingencies provide ample incentives for citizens and officials to engage in a full and free discussion of salient issues. Those in positions of authority are regularly petitioned to acknowledge changing conditions or critical problems. New evidence or new arguments induce government to review its role and form. As a result, there is a constant need to modify the missions and names of public entities as policies are reoriented, programs are reorganized, and new mandates are enacted into law.

The federal government is the nation's foremost collector, classifier, producer, and distributor of information. Virtually all of it is available at little or no charge to those aware of its existence and issuer. However, the cost in time and effort can serve as a deterrent. The multitude of government responsibilities and the magnitude of its organizational structure tend to impede, rather than expedite, public access to informational resources. This tool, which pinpoints subjects, arrays authors, and correlates both, can greatly simplify either a specific search or a general quest for desired data.

At one time or another everyone can profit from some information available from an organizational unit of the federal government. A prime reason for its distribution is to sustain public confidence in governmental performance and to enable recipients to benefit personally from its acquisition. However, the sheer mass of information generated and the profusion of printed and automated tools for retrieving it may discourage many from making an effort to obtain it by rendering

the pursuit more laborious than might otherwise be the case.
A convenient resource is needed that can get the potential
user off to a sure and smooth start.

This volume endeavors to answer two questions: First, over
which aspects of individual, organizational, national, and
international affairs does the U.S. government exert authority
or influence? Second, which units of the federal establishment
are empowered to probe and pursue which matters? This guide
aims to fully cover and to maximize access to the realm of
federal business. Its content and format offer a concise,
yet complete, overview of contemporary public affairs and
governmental policy agents.

The schematic format of this work attempts graphically to
depict existing relationships between public services and
governmental sources. Through the use of a tandem subject
and author approach it enables users to focus promptly on
functions assigned or implied by an official mandate. Its
immediate goal is to assist those who plan to enter and ex-
plore the federal information thicket. Its ultimate goal is
to devise a framework that can be adapted to the dynamic
character of national governance and its information output.

The major difference between this guide and other handbooks
that suggest methods or offer advice on how and where to seek
information from the U.S. government is the use of the concept
of jurisdiction as the central organizational principle. In
this case jurisdiction refers to the tabulation of designated
areas of authority so as to map the routes that may be used to
reach particular informational destinations. A survey of
federal functions, subjects, authors, and sources can be more
thorough and helpful when jurisdiction is employed to link
information needs with information funds.

Though an arrangement based on subject category and issuing
office has its value, such schemes invariably involve some
limitations in scope and depth because of the inclusion of
bibliographic and author data. The purpose of this work is
to clearly and quickly identify topics and specialists so that
users can more precisely match information resources with information deficits. While it may be necessary to consult other
publications for titles and addresses, the need to proceed
through this second stage does not negate the fact that better
preparation during the stage before an inquiry is initiated
has its advantages.

This project is intended to provide comprehensive coverage
of the topics and affairs addressed by all key executive and
legislative branch units of the U.S. government. It identifies
each entity that exercises jurisdiction over a specific subject.
The purpose is to facilitate optimal access to the entire domain
of federal business and the corresponding sources of federal
information. In addition, this guide clarifies and classifies
the effects of concurrent and overlapping authority among
governmental offices. The approach is designed to record and
reveal the relationship between formal powers and official
authors.

The value of such a tool is determined by the selection of
terms to be used. The extensive domain and diversity of federal
jurisdiction would be a major obstacle if it were necessary to
start from scratch. However, this key task is expedited by the
existence of six prominent indexes from which a nearly complete
vocabulary can be compiled. Each is prepared by a different
office for a different purpose. Their complementary nature
enables the limitations of each, however characterized, to be
offset by the merits of the others. These sources are the

latest edition of the GAO Thesaurus, issued by the General
Accounting Office; the Library of Congress subject headings
in the Monthly Catalog of U.S. Government Publications, issued
by the Government Printing Office; the subject index to the
United States Code, issued by the U.S. House of Representatives;
the subject index to the Code of Federal Regulations, issued by
the National Archives and Records Administration; the subject
index to the Statistical Abstract of the United States, issued
by the Census Bureau of the Commerce Department; and the subject
index to CQ Almanac, issued by Congressional Quarterly, Inc.

    Another major feature of this guide is its linkage of subjects
and authors. Several sources were consulted to ascertain these
relationships and to supplement the stock of entries derived from
the indexes cited in the previous paragraph. The key titles are:
CIS/Index, published annually by Congressional Information Service;
Congressional Staff Directory, published semiannually by Congressional Staff Directory, Ltd.; the bound Congressional Record, published annually by the Government Printing Office; Federal Staff
Directory, published semiannually by Congressional Staff Directory,
Ltd.; United States Government Manual, published annually by the
National Archives and Records Administration; and the Washington
Information Directory, published annually by Congressional Quarterly, Inc. The clarity of jurisdictional data and frequency of
subject terms that appear in these publications serve as a solid
foundation for the structure and utility of this manual.

    Because the aims of this project differ from those pursued by
the Government Printing Office, it should be emphasized that the
definition of a government author also differs. The primary
factor used to determine a Government Printing Office author
symbol is the agency imprint or subunit autonomy. Author desig-
nation is linked to the administrative status of its publications.
In this guide the key to authorship is the responsibility to formu
late or implement policy or to monitor or analyze conditions that
pertain to a particular matter. An author is any federal unit
whose mission or status obliges it to create or collect information and to disclose or disseminate it.

    This guide is intended to be used primarily for preliminary
research purposes. However, when information needs concern the
concrete functions of a federal agency, another way exists to
locate the appropriate office. The General Services Administration operates a nationwide network of federal information centers.
These clearinghouses comprise a central source from which guidance
may be obtained regarding all government services, programs, and
regulations. When it is necessary to contact a federal office in
reference to an immediate matter that is of a professional or
personal nature, the nearest federal information center provides
referrals to the government unit that offers relevant information
or tangible assistance. A listing of all centers and their phone
numbers appears in the United States Government Manual, a volume
available at virtually every public library.

    The depository library system is a set of institutions desig-
nated to receive and house U.S. government publications, which
includes those authored by a federal agency, printed at public
expense, or issued as a legal requirement. It is one of the
means intended to inform the public about federal policies and
programs. With certain exceptions, all government publications
are distributed through the Government Printing Office to depository libraries. These collections are located in each state and
congressional district, and the material is available for the
free use of the general public. The nearest depository can be
identified by contacting the local office of a member of Congress.

    The National Technical Information Service is a clearinghouse
for scientific, technical, and engineering information that is

disseminated via government-sponsored research projects. These
reports are prepared by federal agencies, their contractors or
grantees as part of an effort to increase national productivity
and improve international competitiveness. Its collection con-
sists of printed, microform, audiovisual, and electronic products
which are listed and described in databases, indexes, newsletters,
and specialized subscriber services. National Technical Information Service operations are financed by the sale of this material
to the public. Further information may be obtained by contacting:
National Technical Information Service, 5285 Port Royal Road,
Springfield, VA 22161, (703) 487-4650.

An additional way to obtain government information is through
the Freedom of Information Act. It requires public officials to
justify a decision to withhold information from those who submit
a formal request. The Act sets forth standards to determine
which agency records must be released to the public and which
can be kept confidential. It also provides for administrative
and judicial remedies when access is denied. This law applies
to agencies of the executive branch, but not to elected officials
or the federal judiciary. Those who seek material that has not
been published or publicly distributed should consult A Citizen's
Guide On Using The Freedom Of Information Act And The Privacy Act
Of 1974 To Request Government Records, prepared by the House
Government Operations Committee and issued as House Report
103-104, 103rd Congress, 1st Session, 1993. It is available
from the Government Printing Office.

To supplement information available from federal sources with
that disseminated by nonfederal sources one may contact the
National Referral Center. It is a free referral service for
those who have specific questions on any topic. It maintains
a subject-indexed database of some 15,000 organizations that
possess specialized knowledge and are willing to provide information in their area of expertise. The Center is not equipped
to furnish substantive answers or to render bibliographic assistance. In response to requests submitted by mail, phone, or
visit, a reply is usually transmitted within five working days.
Its content includes a list of suggested offices to contact,
including individual names and the type of information services
offered. The address is: National Referral Center, Library of
Congress, John Adams Building, Washington, D.C. 20540, (202)
707-5670.

User Guide

As the consequences of constant change affect public opinion
and debate, elected and appointed officials strive to discern and
address the issues that vex their constituents. To cope with
fluid developments that influence the range of realistic policy
options is to participate in a contest for the imprimatur of
government. This means that the nature and origin of information play a vital role when proposals are being formulated or
programs evaluated.

The perceived obligations and preferred objectives of public
leaders have triggered many important measures to review or reform
federal performance. Ongoing efforts to reorganize or redesignate
offices and to reassign or rearrange duties are a natural reaction
to the political environment. Decisions on institutional status
or title and modified structures or functions always entail corresponding changes in subject dimensions and descriptions.

Subject access is the principal purpose of this guide. An
expanded number of specific subjects flows from additional data
conveyed by various U.S. government publications. The enlarged
listing enhances the prospects of users to find the term that
best meets their needs. A key auxiliary goal is to chart the
linkages among and between subjects, agencies, and committees.

The explanation that follows provides: 1) a review of the
major features of each part, 2) an account of general factors
that concern or pervade the entire project, and 3) a survey of
those relationships that this guide is designed to illuminate.

Part 1 constitutes the core and bulk of this work, from which
most of the other parts are derived. It is an alphabetical in-
ventory of matters that command the attention or require the involvement of the U.S. government. The subject focus is neither
subordinated to, nor restricted by, the inclusion of data readily
available elsewhere. The result is a synoptic introduction to
the roles and tasks assumed by the federal sector. See references are used as guides to broader, narrower or equivalent, but
preferred, terms. Since these references are not repeated elsewhere, it is best to begin a subject search by perusing the left-
hand column of entries and references. Where the precise meaning

of a term is unclear, the numerical code that follows it, which
is correlated with the general categories of Part 2, serves to
clarify its usage by identifying its most salient dimension(s).

The column headings in Part 1 have been abridged. Their full
forms are: Parents = Parent Agencies; Subunits = Agency Subunits;
House = House Committees; Senate = Senate Committees; and Funding =
Appropriations Subcommittees. The order in which parent agencies
are listed in Part 1/Column 2 is not entirely alphabetical. Cabi-
net departments appear first in alphabetical order, next is the
Executive Office of the President when one of its subunits pos-
sesses authority, then all other agencies are entered in alphabetical sequence. This arrangement generally gives a more accu-
rate picture of agency predominance in descending order than would
a strictly alphabetical scheme. It should be emphasized, nonetheless, that this structural relationship does not apply in all cases.

While section 1 of Part 1 employs See references to locate
comparable or commensurate entries, section 2 provides parallel
information in reverse. It lists subjects that are linked with
at least two See references. To discern a useful category is to
identify all other topics covered by the same term. This repre-
sents another way to match alternative forms of related entries
and references.

The interchangeability of two groups of adjectives should also
be noted. For domestic affairs they are: Federal, Government,
National, and Public; for global affairs they are: Foreign, International, Overseas, and World. When it occurs that one of these
words could be the first half of a specific subject category, a
glance at the pages of Part 1/Section 1 that list such terms
might expedite a search.

Part 2 groups the specific entries of Part 1 under 20 general
subject headings. This is an effort to produce a refined list of
subject categories unaffected by the historical and political
factors that shape agency and committee jurisdiction. It is also
intended to aid those whose information needs cover a wide range
of related activities, their multiple aspects, and mutual effects.
Another aim is to eliminate the need for See also references in
Part 1, since related terms are clustered for a more convenient
overview of a broad policy sphere. The interdependent nature of,
and shared assignment over, many responsibilities means that
numerous terms appear under more than one general subject heading.
Part 1 should be consulted to identify entities having jurisdiction
over each entry in Part 2.

Since the terms in Part 1 do not include all possible variations
under which a given subject may be entered, the following expedient
may be helpful when a certain term is not listed. First, determine
which of the general subject categories of Part 2 is most likely to
cover the specific topic that is being researched. Then scan the
entries under that heading in section 1 to ascertain which most
closely matches the meaning of the one at hand.

Parts 3 and 4 are aimed at those for whom an administrative
agency or congressional committee approach is convenient or necessary. The second section of Parts 2-5 each chart some associated
relationships that merit attention in the context of federal inter-
action and information. They correlate authors to fill potential
gaps that can stem from a straight subject survey. Although this
might result in some repetition, on the whole it contributes to
easier retrieval of and simplified searching for desired data.

Part 5 affirms that Appropriations Committee hearings are a
major source of information on all aspects of public activity.
In a technical sense the appropriations panels do not exercise
authority over substantive policy since their jurisdiction is

based on agency budgets rather than subject areas. However, the focus on past and proposed spending necessarily entails an examination of program management and output which yields an information product that supplements more topically oriented ones. The appropriations subcommittee structure is identical in each house of Congress.

In addition to its normal use, the Index serves some additional purposes. Some agency subunits exercise authority over more subject areas than some parent agencies. These major subunits can be identified by noting the page number references to Part 1. The Index can also be used to compile a list of subunits for major parent agencies; to match agency subunits with congressional committees when more than one panel exercises jurisdiction over a single agency; and to facilitate the isolation, combination, or comparison of certain entities to meet particular research needs.

An important feature of federal jurisdiction is the partition of authority between or among offices based on some traditional or natural divisions of many subject categories. Those pairs of concepts that most commonly bisect a domain or function are its public/private, domestic/international, civil/military, financial/substantive, regulatory/research, or policy/agency components. In the large majority of cases, which office exercises jurisdiction over which components is comparatively clear.

Where the distinction between components is not evident, the citation of certain committees provides a key clue. For the first dichotomy, the House Government Reform and Oversight and Senate Governmental Affairs committees indicate a public element; for the second, the House International Relations and Senate Foreign Relations committees indicate an international one; for the third, the House National Security and Senate Armed Services committees indicate a military one; for the fourth, the House Ways and Means and Senate Finance committees indicate a financial one. For the fifth, it is necessary to recognize those agencies that are primarily research units. These include the four congressional support agencies (Congressional Budget Office, General Accounting Office, Library of Congress, Office of Technology Assessment), three subunits of the Executive Office of the President (Council of Economic Advisers, Council on Environmental Quality, Science and Technology Policy Office), two independent entities (National Science Foundation and Smithsonian Institution), two subunits of the Commerce Department (Census Bureau and National Institute of Standards and Technology), and one subunit of the Health and Human Services Department (National Institutes of Health). The last dichotomy is most clearly reflected in the division of responsibility between the appropriations panels and all other committees, while the House Government Reform and Oversight and Senate Governmental Affairs committees may examine a matter from either perspective.

There are several committees and agencies whose jurisdiction encompasses nearly the entire spectrum of federal activities. Nonetheless in this guide they are listed only under those subject areas in which they play a prominent role. That they may issue valuable information relating to matters that might not be automatically associated with their title is a fact that should not be overlooked. These units include the Appropriations and Budget committees in both houses of Congress, the House Government Reform and Oversight and Ways and Means committees, the Senate Finance and Governmental Affairs committees, and the first three congressional support agencies cited in the previous paragraph.

Certain classes of units are not listed in this guide. Entities that focus solely on such internal affairs as administrative efficiency, budgets, personnel, and legal matters lack

substantive jurisdiction and do not warrant inclusion. Those
offices with only a subsidiary or subordinate interest in a given
subject area are omitted because of their limited involvement or
responsibility. Interim bodies are excluded because their brief
existence outweighs their role as government authors in a roster
of permanent units. Advisory panels are not cited because their
information products are channeled through the offices with which
they are formally affiliated. Government corporations, though
sponsored and monitored by executive branch agencies, are privately
owned and mainly privately funded. Their legal and financial status
bar them from membership in the family of federal authors.

In the legislative branch, congressional subcommittees, except
for the appropriations panels, are not named. This is because of
their susceptibility to reorganization or redesignation and because
citations to legislative information are usually made to the full
committee. Also omitted are party organs and legislative caucuses.
The former are partisan bodies or leadership positions and the
latter are informal groups or state delegations. Though neither
exercises legal authority, both customarily exert political
influence.

Other than the opinions issued by specific courts, there are
basically three authors that comprise the federal judiciary. One
is the Judicial Conference of the United States, which is the
policymaking arm of the judiciary and is chaired by the Chief
Justice of the U.S. Another is the Administrative Office of the
United States Courts, which is responsible for monitoring and
managing judicial administration and preparing reports on workload,
resources, practices, and results. One other is the Federal
Judicial Center, which was created to meet the research and educational needs of the judiciary. Although not otherwise cited in
this guide, their publications cover all aspects of the national
court system and the matters under its jurisdiction. The large
majority of those subjects addressed by judicial authors appears
in Part 2/Section 1 under the heading of Legal Affairs.

The absence of a subject index is a by-product of features that
characterize Parts 1 and 2. The alphabetical listing of specific
subject categories in Part 1 corresponds to such an index. The
numerical codes that appear after the terms in Part 1, when com-
bined with the entries under columns 2, 4, 5, and 6, serve as a
guide to the same specific subject categories in section 1 of
Parts 2-5. The organization of Part 2/Section 1 affords a wider
frame of reference from which to search for narrower and more
cogent terms.

The relationships that form the body of this guide are listed
below. Each pair of terms is followed by a statement about how
to link them when one starts with the item on the left. It is a
tabular summary of uses that presents an overview of information
purposes served and research options addressed.

Specific Subject
    General Subject: Part 1/Column 1, then match numerical codes
                     with codes in Part 2/Section 1.
    Parent Agency: Part 1/Column 2.
    Legislative Committee: Part 1/Columns 4 & 5.
    Appropriations Subcommittee: Part 1/Column 6.

General Subject
    Specific Subject: Part 2/Section 1.
    Parent Agency: Part 2/Section 2/Column 2.
    Legislative Committee: Part 2/Section 2/Columns 3 & 4.
    Appropriations Subcommittee: Part 2/Section 2/Column 5.

Parent Agency
    Specific Subject: Part 3/Section 1.
    General Subject: Part 3/Section 2, then match numerical codes
                    with codes in Part 2/Section 1 or 2.
    Legislative Committee: Part 3/Section 2/Columns 2 & 3.
    Appropriations Subcommittee: Part 3/Section 2/Column 4.

Legislative Committee
    Specific Subject: Part 4/Section 1.
    General Subject: Part 4/Section 2, then match numerical codes
                    with codes in Part 2/Section 1 or 2.
    Parent Agency: Part 4/Section 2/Column 2.
    Appropriations Subcommittee: Part 4/Section 2/Column 4.

Appropriations Subcommittee
    Specific Subject: Part 5/Section 1.
    General Subject: Part 5/Section 2, then match numerical codes
                    with codes in Part 2/Section 1 or 2.
    Parent Agency: Part 5/Section 2/Column 2.
    Legislative Committee: Part 5/Section 2/Columns 3 & 4.

Accessing U.S. Government Information, Revised and Expanded Edition

Part 1

Specific Subject Categories

EXECUTIVE AND LEGISLATIVE JURISDICTION BY SPECIFIC SUBJECT CATEGORY

	PARENTS	SUBUNITS	HOUSE	SENATE	FUNDING
Abortion (11, 14)	HHS	PHS	CO, JU	JU, LA	LAB
Abuse of authority. See Inspectors General					
Accidents. See Aviation safety, Highway safety, Marine safety, Occupational safety, Product safety, Railroad safety					
Accounting (9, 10)	TRE TRE EOP GAO	FMS IRS OMB	CO GR WM	BA FI GA	COM TRE
Acid rain (8, 16)	EOP EPA	CEQ	CO	EP	VA
Acquired immune deficiency syndrome (AIDS) (11)	HHS HHS HHS HHS HHS	CDC FDA HRSA NIAI NIDA	CO	LA	LAB
Addiction. See Alcoholism, Drug abuse, Smoking					
Additives. See Food Inspection					
Administrative law (10, 14)	ACUS		GR, JU	GA, JU	TRE
Administrative management. See Federal paperwork, Inspectors General, Public administration					
Admiralty law. See International law, Maritime industry, Salvage					
Adoption. See Family services					
Adult education (5)	EDU EDU	PE VAE	EE	LA	LAB
Advertising (2, 3)	HHS TRE FCC FTC SEC	FDA ATF	BA, CO	BA, CO	COM
Advisory committees (10)	GSA	CMS	GR	GA	TRE
Aeronautics (17, 19)	EOP NASA SI	STP	SC	CO	VA
Aerospace industry. See Government procurement					
Affirmative action. See Civil rights					

	PARENTS	SUBUNITS	HOUSE	SENATE	FUNDING
Aged (12, 18)	HHS HHS SSA	AA NIA	CO EE WM	AGI FI LA	LAB
Agricultural credit (1, 9, 12)	AGR AGR FCA	FAHA REA	AG	AG	AGR
Agricultural development (1, 4, 13)	AGR AGR AGR	ACS ES ICD	AG	AG	AGR
Agricultural markets (1, 13)	AGR AGR	AMS FAS	AG	AG	AGR
Agricultural production (1)	AGR AGR	AMS ASCS	AG	AG	AGR
Agricultural research (1, 17)	AGR AGR	ARS NAL	AG SC	AG	AGR
Agricultural subsidies (1, 12)	AGR AGR	ASCS CCC	AG	AG	AGR
Agricultural surpluses (1, 13, 18)	AGR AGR AGR	CCC FAS FNS	AG	AG	AGR
Aid to Families with Dependent Children (AFDC). See Welfare					
Air Force. See Armed forces					
Air pollution (8, 11, 16, 17)	COM TRA EPA	NOAA FAA	CO SC	EP	COM VA
Aircraft. See Aviation safety					
Airlines. See Aviation industry					
Airports (4, 19)	TRA	FAA	TR	CO	TRA
Airspace (13, 15)	DEF STA STA	AF LAO PMA	IR NS	AR FR	COM
Alcoholic beverages (2, 14)	TRE	ATF	CO JU	CO JU	TRE
Alcoholism (11)	HHS	NIAA	CO	LA	LAB
Aliens (6, 14)	JUS LAB LAB	INS ETA ILA	EE JU	JU LA	COM LAB
Allergies (11)	HHS	NIAI	CO	LA	LAB
American history. See Federal records, Historic preserva- tion, Museums					
Animals (11, 16)	AGR HHS INT SI	APHIS FDA FWS	AG RE	AG EP	AGR INT

	PARENTS	SUBUNITS	HOUSE	SENATE	FUNDING
Astronomy (17)	DEF NASA NSF	NAVO	SC	CO	VA
Athletics. See Sports					
Atmosphere (8, 17)	COM TRA EPA NASA NSF	NOAA FAA	CO SC	CO EP	COM VA
Atomic energy. See Nuclear energy					
Audio equipment. See Recording industry					
Auditing. See Accounting					
Authors. See Copyrights					
Automation. See Industrial technology					
Automobile industry (2, 11, 19)	TRA EPA FTC	NHTSA	CO TR	CO EP	COM TRA
Aviation industry (2, 19)	TRA NMB	FAA	CO SC TR	CO EP	TRA
Aviation safety (11, 17)	TRA NTSB	FAA	TR	CO	TRA
Bacteriology (11)	HHS	NIAI	CO	LA	LAB
Balance of payments. See Trade deficits					
Bank deposits (9)	TRE FDIC	TSO	BA	BA	TRE VA
Bank notes. See Currency					
Bank regulation (9)	TRE FHFB FRB	CC	BA	BA	TRE VA
Bank reserves. See Money supply					
Bankruptcy (9, 14)	JUS JUS SEC	CID EUST	JU	JU	COM
Beaches. See Recreation areas					
Bicameralism. See Congressional organization					
Bicycles. See Product safety					
Bilingual education (5)	EDU	BE	EE	LA	LAB
Bill of Rights. See Eminent domain, Juries, Legal services, Privacy, Sentences, Trials					

	PARENTS	SUBUNITS	HOUSE	SENATE	FUNDING
Billboards (2, 3)	TRA	FEHA	TR	EP	TRA
Biotechnology (17)	COM	NIST	CO	CO	COM
	HHS	FDA	SC	LA	LAB
	HHS	NIAI			
	HHS	NIGM			
	EOP	STP			
	NSF				
	OTA				
Birds (16)	AGR	APHIS	AG	AG	AGR
	INT	FWS	RE	EP	INT

Birth control. See Abortion,
  Family planning, Population
  growth

Birth defects. See
  Prenatal care

Birth rates. See Health data

Black market. See
  Commercial law

Blindness. See Disability
  benefits, Handicapped,
  Visual disorders

Blood (11)	HHS	FDA	CO	LA	LAB
	HHS	NHL			

Boating. See Marine safety

Bonds. See Government
  securities, Public debt,
  Securities industry

Border patrol (13, 14)	JUS	INS	IR	FR	COM
	TRE	CS	JU	JU	TRE

Borrowing. See Commercial
  credit, Consumer credit,
  Government borrowing

Boundaries. See International
  boundaries, State boundaries,
  Territories

Brain disorders. See Handicapped, Mental health,
  Neurological diseases

Brand names. See Trademarks

Breathing disorders. See
  Respiratory diseases

Bridges (4, 19)	TRA	CG	TR	EP	TRA
	TRA	FEHA			
	TRA	FRA			
Broadcasting (2, 3)	COM	NTIA	CO	CO	COM
	FCC				

Brokerage firms. See
  Securities industry

	PARENTS	SUBUNITS	HOUSE	SENATE	FUNDING
Budget administration (9, 10)	TRE	FMS	AP	AP	TRE
	EOP	OMB	GR	FI	
	GAO		WM	GA	
Budget deficits (9, 10)	TRE	PDB	BU	BU	TRE
	EOP	NEC	WM	FI	
	EOP	OMB			
	CBO				
Budget formulation (9, 10)	TRE	EPO	BU	BU	TRE
	EOP	CEA	GR	GA	
	EOP	OMB	RU		
	CBO				
Building standards (11, 17, 20)	COM	NIST	BA	BA	COM
	HUD	MHS	SC	CO	VA
Burn injuries (11)	HHS	NIGM	CO	LA	LAB
Bus lines (2, 19)	ICC		CO	CO	TRA
Business assistance (2, 4)	COM	EDA	BA	BA	COM
	TRA	FRA	SB	EP	TRA
	TRA	MA	TR	SB	
	EXIM				
	FEMA				
	SBA				

Business investment (9)	COM	EAB	BA	BA	COM
	TRE	IRS	CO	CO	TRE
	EOP	NEC	SB	FI	
	SBA		WM	SB	
	SEC				
Business regulation (2)	FCC		CO	CO	COM
	FTC		SB	SB	
	ICC			(JEC)	
	SBA				

	PARENTS	SUBUNITS	HOUSE	SENATE	FUNDING
Cancer (11)	HHS	NCI	CO	LA	LAB
Capital formation. See Business investment					
Capital punishment (14)	JUS	PDO	JU	JU	COM
Capitol facilities (10)	ARC		HO, TR	EP, RU	LEG
Cardiology. See Heart disease					
Cargo. See Freight					
Cartography. See Mapping					
Catastrophic illness. See Health insurance					
Censorship. See Government information					
Census (10)	COM	CB	GR	GA	COM
Certificates of deposit. See Bank deposits.					
Charitable organizations (3, 18)	TRE PS	IRS	GR WM	FI GA	TRE
Checking accounts. See Money supply					
Checks. See Negotiable instruments					
Chemicals (11, 17)	COM LAB EPA NSF OTA	NIST OSHA	CO EE	CO LA	COM VA
Chief Justice. See Federal judges					
Child abduction. See Missing children					
Child abuse (10)	HHS	CYFA	EE	LA	LAB
Child care. See Day care					
Child custody. See Family services					
Child health (11, 18)	HHS HHS HHS	DDA MCHRD NICH	CO	LA	LAB
Child labor (6)	LAB	ESA	EE	LA	LAB
Child nutrition (18)	AGR	FNS	AG, EE	AG	AGR
Child support (12, 18)	HHS TRE	CSE IRS	EE WM	FI LA	LAB
Childbirth. See Prenatal care					
Cities. See Local governments					

	PARENTS	SUBUNITS	HOUSE	SENATE	FUNDING
Citizens abroad (13)	STA STA	CAB LAO	IR	FR	COM
Citizens band radio. See Telecommunications					
Citizenship (10, 14)	JUS STA	INS CAB	JU	JU	COM
Civil defense (15)	DEF TRA TRA FEMA	DCPA CG ETO	NS	AR	DEF VA
Civil disorders (14)	JUS JUS FEMA	FBI MS	JU	JU	COM
Civil procedure (14)	JUS	PDO	JU	JU	COM
Civil rights (14)	JUS CRC	CRD	JU	JU	COM
Civil Service. See Government employees					
Civil-military relations (10)	EOP LC	NSC CRS	IR JU	FR JU	TRE
Class action. See Civil procedure					
Classified information. See Government information					
Climate. See Atmosphere, Environmental research, Weather					
Coal (7, 8, 16)	ENR ENR INT INT INT INT	ERA FEO GS LMB MMS SMRE	CO RE SC	EN EP	ENER INT
Coastal zone management (16, 17)	COM DEF	NOAA ACE	RE	CO EN	COM
Cocaine. See Drug abuse, Drug testing, Drug traffic					
Coinage. See Currency					
Coins. See Numismatics					
Collective bargaining. See Labor relations					
Colleges. See Higher education					
Combat readiness. See Armed forces					
Commander in Chief. See Presidency					
Commemorative medals. See Numismatics					

	PARENTS	SUBUNITS	HOUSE	SENATE	FUNDING
Commercial credit (2, 9)	TRE EOP FRB	CC NEC	BA (JEC)	BA	COM
Commercial law (2, 14)	JUS FTC ICC	CID	BA, CO, JU, SB	BA, CO, JU, SB (JEC)	COM
Commercial paper. See Negotiable instruments					
Commodity markets (1, 2)	CFTC		AG	AG	AGR
Communicable diseases (11)	HHS HHS HHS	CDC HRSA NIAI	CO	LA	LAB
Community service. See Volunteer services					
Compensation. See Fringe benefits, Pensions, Wages					
Compensatory education (5)	EDU EDU	CEP PE	EE	LA	LAB
Computer crime. See White collar crime					
Computer security (14, 17)	COM JUS EOP GSA	NIST CRID OMD IRMS	GR JU GO	GA JU	COM TRE
Computer technology (3, 17)	COM EOP GSA NSF OTA	NIST STP IRMS	GR SC	CO GA	COM VA
Condominiums. See Housing management					
Confidential data. See Privacy					
Confirmations. See Congressional power					

Conflicts of interest. See
  Government ethics, Judicial
  ethics, Members of Congress					

Congressional agenda. See
  Elections, Lobbying,
  Presidency					

Congressional districts (10)	COM JUS	CB CRD	JU	JU	COM
Congressional employees (6, 10)	JUS JUS	CID CRID	HO	RU	LEG
Congressional ethics. See Members of Congress					
Congressional operations (10)	GAO LC	CRS	GR, HO, RU	GA RU	LEG
Congressional organization (10)	LC	CRS	GR, RU	GA, RU	LEG

	PARENTS	SUBUNITS	HOUSE	SENATE	FUNDING
Congressional oversight (10)	GAO		GR	GA	LEG
	LC	CRS	RU	RU	
Congressional power (10, 14)	JUS	AG	JU	JU	LEG
	LC	CRS			
Congressional-executive	JUS	LCO	GR	FR	LEG
relations (10, 14)	EOP	OMB	IR	GA	TRE
	GAO		JU	JU	
	LC	CRS	RU	RU	

Consent decrees. See
  Court orders

Conservation. See Energy
  conservation, Environmental
  protection, Land management,
  Soil conservation, Wilderness
  areas, Wildlife conservation

Constituent services. See
  Members of Congress

	PARENTS	SUBUNITS	HOUSE	SENATE	FUNDING
Constitutional amendments (14)	JUS	AG	JU	JU	COM, LEG

Constitutional litigation.
  See Federal courts

Constitutional structure.
  See Separation of powers

	PARENTS	SUBUNITS	HOUSE	SENATE	FUNDING
Construction industry (11, 20)	HUD	UDAG	BA	BA	VA
	HUD	URO	EE	LA	
	LAB	OSHA			

Consulates. See
  Diplomatic service

	PARENTS	SUBUNITS	HOUSE	SENATE	FUNDING
Consumer credit (9, 14)	TRE	CC	BA	BA	COM
	EOP	NEC	CO	CO	
	FDIC				
	FHFB				
	FRB				
	FTC				
	NCUA				
Consumer education (5)	AGR	ARS	AG	AG	COM
	HHS	FDA	CO	CO	VA
	CPSC		GR	GA	
	FTC				
	GSA	CIC			
Consumer Price Index (2, 9)	LAB	LSB	EE (JEC)	LA	LAB
Consumer protection (2, 11)	CPSC		CO	CO	COM
	FTC				VA

Consumer spending.
  See Economic data

Contamination. See Food
  inspection, Toxic sub-
  stances, Water pollution

Contempt power. See Administrative law, Congressional
  power, Federal courts

	PARENTS	SUBUNITS	HOUSE	SENATE	FUNDING
Continental shelf. See Outer continental shelf					
Contracts. See Government contracts, Inspectors General, Public administration					
Cooperative housing. See Housing management					
Copyrights (3, 14)	STA ITC LC OTA	EBA COPY	JU	JU	COM
Corporate finance. See Bankruptcy, Business investment, Foreign taxes, International finance, Securities industry, Taxation					
Corporate mergers. See Antitrust law					
Corporate structure. See Commercial law					
Correctional facilities (14)	JUS JUS JUS	JAB NIC PB	JU	JU	COM
Correspondence courses (2, 5)	EDU VA FTC PS	VAE VBA	CO EE	CO LA	COM LAB
Corrupt practices (10, 14)	JUS JUS	CRID EUSA	HO JU	ET JU	COM LEG
Cosmetics industry (11)	HHS	FDA	CO	CO, LA	AGR
Cotton. See Fibers					
Counterfeiting (14)	TRE TRE	EPB SS	JU	JU	TRE
Counterintelligence. See Intelligence activities					
Counties. See Local governments					
Court costs. See Civil procedure					
Court employees. See Judicial administration					
Court orders (14)	JUS JUS	CID MS	JU	JU	COM
Court records. See Judicial administration					
Court rules. See Federal courts					

	PARENTS	SUBUNITS	HOUSE	SENATE	FUNDING
Courts-martial. See Military law					
Covert action. See Intelligence activities					
Credit bureaus. See Consumer protection					
Credit cards. See Consumer credit					
Credit programs (4, 9, 20)	TRE TRE EOP EOP CBO	DFO FMS NEC OMB	AP BA BU	AP BA BU	TRE
Credit unions (9)	FRB NCUA		BA	BA	VA
Crime data (14)	JUS JUS	FBI JSB	JU	JU	COM
Crime prevention (5)	JUS JUS	JAB NIJ	JU	JU	COM
Crime victims (12, 14)	JUS JUS JUS FEMA	EUSA JAB JPO	BA JU	BA JU	COM
Criminal investigations. See Law enforcement					
Criminal procedure (14)	JUS	PDO	JU	JU	COM
Criminals. See Prisoners					
Crops (1, 12)	AGR AGR	ARS FCIC	AG	AG	AGR
Cultural exchange. See International agreements					
Cultural expression. See Arts, Humanities, Non-profit organizations					
Currency (9, 10)	TRE TRE TRE TRE FRB	CC EPB MINT TUS	BA	BA	TRE
Customs (9, 13)	COM TRE EOP ITC	IMP CS TRO	IR WM	FI FR	COM TRE
Dairy industry (1)	AGR AGR AGR	AMS ASCS FSIS	AG	AG	AGR
Dams (4, 16)	DEF INT TVA	ACE RB	RE TR	EN EP	ENER

	PARENTS	SUBUNITS	HOUSE	SENATE	FUNDING
Data banks. See Privacy					
Data collection. See Federal paperwork					
Day care (6, 18)	HHS	CHB	EE	FI	LAB
	HHS	FAO	WM	LA	
	LAB	WB			
	TRE	IRS			
Deafness. See Disability benefits, Handicapped, Hearing disorders					
Death penalty. See Capital punishment					
Debt collection (9)	JUS	EUSA	CO	CO	COM
	TRE	FMS	EE	FI	TRE
	TRE	IRS	JU	JU	
	EOP	OMB			
	FTC				
	GAO				
Debt management (9, 10)	TRE	DFO	WM	FI	TRE
	TRE	FFB			
	TRE	PDB			
	EOP	NEC			
	GAO				
Deceptive practices. See Consumer protection					
Declaratory judgments. See Judicial remedies					
Defaults. See Bankruptcy, Debt collection, Fore-closure					
Defective products. See Product safety					
Defense industry. See Government procurement					
Deficit financing. See Budget deficits, Debt management, Government borrowing					
Demographic data. See Census					
Dentistry (11)	HHS	NID	CO	LA	LAB
Deportation (14)	JUS	INS	JU	JU	COM
Deposit insurance. See Bank deposits					
Depressed areas (4, 20)	COM	EDA	BA	BA	COM
	HUD	BGA	TR	EP	VA
Depression. See Mental health					
Detention. See Border patrol, Criminal pro-cedure, Extradition					

	PARENTS	SUBUNITS	HOUSE	SENATE	FUNDING
Devaluation. See International finance					
Developing countries. See Foreign aid					
Diamonds. See Precious stones					
Diet. See Nutrition					
Digestive diseases. See Eating disorders					
Diplomatic immunity (13, 14)	JUS STA STA	LCO LAO PO	IR JU	FR JU	COM
Diplomatic recognition (13)	STA STA EOP	PMA PO NSC	IR	FR	COM
Diplomatic service (10, 13)	STA STA STA	FMO FSE PO	IR	FR	COM
Disability benefits (12, 18)	VA SSA	VBA	EE VA	LA VA	LAB VA
Disabled. See Handicapped					
Disarmament. See Arms control					
Disaster relief (4, 12, 13)	AGR FEMA IDCA SBA	FAHA AID	AG IR SB TR	AG EP FR SB	AGR VA
Discount rate. See Interest rates					
Discrimination (14)	EDU HHS HUD LAB EEOC	CRO CRO FHEO CRO	BA CO EE JU	BA CO JU LA	COM LAB
Disease control. See Epidemiology					
Displaced persons. See Disaster relief, Foreign aid, Refugees					
District courts. See Federal courts					
District of Columbia (10, 20)	NCPC PADC		AP, GR, RE, TR	AP, EP, GA	DC
Dividends. See Taxation					
Domestic violence. See Family services					
Draft. See Selective Service					
Drinking water. See Water supply					

	PARENTS	SUBUNITS	HOUSE	SENATE	FUNDING
Drought. See Crops					
Drug abuse (11, 18)	HHS	NIDA	CO	LA	LAB
Drug safety (11, 17)	HHS	FDA	CO	LA	AGR
	OTA				
Drug testing (6, 11, 17)	DEF	HAO	CO	AR	LAB
	HHS	NIDA	GR	CO	TRE
	LAB	LMR	NS	GA	
	EOP	STP		LA	
	OPM				
	OTA				
Drug traffic (13, 14)	DEF	CCCI	IR	FR	COM
	JUS	CRID	JU	JU	TRE
	JUS	DEA			
	JUS	FBI			
	JUS	INS			
	JUS	INTER			
	JUS	JAB			
	STA	INM			
	TRA	CG			
	TRE	CS			
	EOP	NDC			

Drunk driving. See
 Highway safety

Earned income credit.
 See Taxation

Earth sciences. See
 Atmosphere, Geology,
 Oceanography

Earthquake damage. See
 Disaster relief

	PARENTS	SUBUNITS	HOUSE	SENATE	FUNDING
Earthquake research (8, 17)	INT	GS	RE	CO	INT
	NSF		SC	EP	
Eating disorders (11)	HHS	NIDD	CO	LA	LAB

Ecological risk. See
 Global environment

	PARENTS	SUBUNITS	HOUSE	SENATE	FUNDING
Economic controls (2, 9)	TRD	EPO	BA	BA	TRE
	EOP	CEA			
	EOP	NEC			
Economic data (1, 2, 6, 9)	AGR	ERS	AG	AG	AGR
	AGR	NASS	BA	BA	COM
	COM	CB	BU	BU	LAB
	COM	KAB	EE	LA	
	COM	IEB	(JEC)		
	LAB	LSB			
	EOP	CEA			
	CBO				
	FRB				
	ITC				
	SBA				
	SEC				

Education assistance. See
 Student loans, Veterans,
 Vocational education

	PARENTS	SUBUNITS	HOUSE	SENATE	FUNDING
Education data (5)	EDU	NCES	EE	LA	LAB
Education research (5)	EDU EDU	ERI NIE	EE	LA	LAB
Elderly. See Aged					
Elections (10)	JUS FEC	CRID	HO JU	JU RU	LEG TRE
Electric power (7, 17)	ENR TVA	FERC	CO, RE, SC, TR	EN EP	ENER
Electrical standards (17)	COM NSF	NIST	SC	CO	COM
Electronic data processing. See Computer technology					
Electronic fund transfers. See Financial institutions					
Electronic surveillance. See Privacy					
Elementary education (5)	EDU	ESE	EE	LA	LAB
Embargoes. See Exports					
Embassies. See Diplomatic service					
Emergency preparedness. See Civil defense					
Eminent domain (10, 14)	JUS TRE	LNR IRS	GR TR	EP GA	COM
Employee benefits. See Fringe benefits					
Employer liability. See Workers compensation					
Employment data. See Economic data					
Endangered species (16)	AGR AGR COM INT	APHIS FS NOAA FWS	RE SC	CO EP	COM INT
Energy conservation (7, 17)	COM ENR HUD	NIST CRE EEO	CO	EN	ENER
Energy consumption (2, 7)	ENR ENR	ERA FERC	CO	EN	ENER INT
Energy data (7)	ENR	EIA	CO	EN	INT
Energy prices (2, 7)	ENR ENR	ERA FERC	CO	EN	ENER INT
Energy production (2, 7, 17)	ENR INT EOP OTA	FERC MMS STP	CO RE	EN	ENER INT

	PARENTS	SUBUNITS	HOUSE	SENATE	FUNDING
Energy research (7, 17)	ENR INT EOP NSF OTA	ERO GS STP	CO RE SC	EN	ENER INT
Energy reserves. See Resource shortages					
Energy storage (7, 8)	ENR ENR EPA	CRE ESH	CO	EN	ENER VA

Engineering. See Computer
  technology, Industrial
  technology, Technology
  transfer					

Entertainment industry. See
  Broadcasting, Copyrights,
  Recording industry					

Entitlement programs. See
  Food stamps, Health insur-
  ance, Pensions, Social
  Security, Unemployment
  compensation, Welfare					

Environmental liability (2, 11, 14)	JUS EPA NTSB	LNR	CO SC TR	EP	TRA VA
Environmental protection (8, 11)	AGR COM INT EPA	FS NOAA FWS	CO RE	EN EP	INT VA
Environmental research (8, 17)	COM ENR HHS HUD STA EOP EPA NSF OTA	NOAA ESH NIEH EEO OIE CEQ	RE SC	CO EP	COM VA
Epidemiology (11)	HHS	CDC	CO	LA	LAB
Equal time. See Broadcasting					
Equitable relief. See Judicial remedies					
Espionage (13, 14)	JUS JUS EOP	CRID FBI CIA	IR JU	FR JU	COM DEF
Estates and trusts. See Taxation					
Estuaries. See Coastal zone management					
Ethnic groups (5,10)	COM INT JUS SI	CB IAB CRD	CO JU	CO JU	COM

	PARENTS	SUBUNITS	HOUSE	SENATE	FUNDING
Exchange rates. See Foreign currency					
Excises. See Taxation					
Executive agreements. See International agreements					
Executive branch operations (10)	EOP GAO GSA	OMB	AP GR	AP GA	TRE
Executive branch organization (10)	EOP	OMB	GR	GA	TRE
Executive orders (10, 14)	JUS EOP NARA	LCO OMB	GR JU	GA JU	TRE
Executive power. See Presidency					
Executive privilege (10, 14)	JUS EOP	AG WHO	GR JU	GA JU	COM TRE
Expatriation (14)	JUS STA	CID CAB	IR JU	FR JU	COM
Expenditures. See Government spending					
Exploration. See Space exploration, Underground exploration, Undersea exploration					
Explosives (11, 14, 17)	LAB TRE CPSC	MSHA ATF	EE JU SC	CO JU LA	COM TRE
Exports (2, 13)	AGR COM DEF ENR STA TRE EOP EXIM IDCA ITC SBA	FAS EXP DTSA DPO EBA CS TRO TDA	AG BA CO IR SB	AG BA CO FR SB	COM FO
Expositions (2, 13)	COM USIA	ITA	CO IR	CO FR	COM
Extradition (13, 14)	JUS JUS STA STA	CRID INTER LAO LEI	IR JU	FR JU	COM
Eye care. See Visual disorders					
Factories. See Industrial pollution, Labor standards, Occupational safety					
Family farms. See Agricultural credit					

	PARENTS	SUBUNITS	HOUSE	SENATE	FUNDING
Family planning (18)	HHS HHS	HRSA PHS	CO	LA	LAB
Family services (18)	HHS HHS SSA	CYFA FYS	EE	LA	LAB
Farm labor. See Migrant workers					
Farming. See Agricul- tural development					
Federal charters (14)	GSA JUS TRE	CMS CID CC	BA GR JU	BA GA JU	COM TRE
Federal courts (10, 14)	JUS JUS JUS	LCO PDO SG	JU	JU	COM
Federal judges (10, 14)	JUS	AG	JU	JU	COM
Federal paperwork (10)	TRE EOP	IRS OMB	GR WM	FI GA	TRE
Federal property (10)	GSA GSA	FPR FSS	GR	GA	TRE
Federal records (3, 10)	LC NARA		GR HO	GA RU	TRE
Federalism. See Inter- governmental relations					
Felonies. See Crime data					
Ferries. See Water transportation					
Fibers (1)	AGR AGR	AMS ASCS	AG	AG	AGR
Financial institutions (9)	TRE TRE TRE EOP FDIC FHFB FRB NCUA SEC	CC DFO TSO NEC	BA (JEC)	BA	TRE VA

Financial management. See
  Budget administration,
  Debt collection,
  Inspectors General					

Financial markets. See Securities industry					
Fire control (16, 17)	AGR COM FEMA	FS NIST	AG SC	AG CO	COM
Fire damage. See Disaster relief					
Firearms (14)	TRE	ATF	JU	JU	COM TRE

	PARENTS	SUBUNITS	HOUSE	SENATE	FUNDING
Fiscal policy. See Government borrowing, Government spending, Taxation					
Fish. See Wildlife conservation					
Fishing. See Maritime industry					
Flag of the U.S. (10)	EOP	WHO	JU	JU	TRE
Flammable materials. See Product safety					
Flood control (8, 16)	AGR COM DEF INT TVA	SCS NOAA ACE RB	AG RE TR	AG EN EP	AGR ENER
Flood damage. See Disaster relief					
Flowers. See Horticulture					
Food distribution (13, 18)	AGR AGR	FAS FNS	AG EE	AG	AGR
Food inspection (11)	AGR COM HHS	FSIS NOAA FDA	AG CO	AG LA	AGR
Food production. See Agricultural production					
Food stamps (12)	AGR	FNS	AG	AG	AGR
Foreclosure (9, 14)	AGR HUD HUD HUD	FAHA FEHO MHP SHP	AG BA	AG BA	AGR VA
Foreign agents (13, 14)	JUS	CRID	JU	FR	COM
Foreign aid (13)	AGR STA TRE EOP IDCA	FAS IFD DNO NEC AID	IR	FR	COM FO
Foreign currency (9, 13)	TRE EOP FRB	IMA NEC	BA	BA	TRE
Foreign debts. See International finance					
Foreign investments (2, 9, 13)	COM STA TRE	ITA EBA TIP	BA, CO, IR, WM (JEC)	BA FI FR	COM
Foreign markets. See Exports					
Foreign products. See Imports					
Foreign property (13)	TRE	FACO	IR	FR	TRE
Foreign residents. See Aliens					

	PARENTS	SUBUNITS	HOUSE	SENATE	FUNDING
Foreign service. See Diplomatic service					
Foreign sovereign immunity (13, 14)	STA	LAO	JU	JU	COM
Foreign taxes (9, 13)	TRE TRE EOP	INTA IRS NEC	WM	FI	TRE
Foreign visitors (13)	JUS STA STA USIA	INS CAB ECA	IR JU	FR JU	COM
Forestry (16)	AGR INT TVA	FS LMB	AG RE	AG EN	INT
Forged documents. See Identity papers					
Foster care. See Family services					
Foundations. See Non-profit organizations					
Franchises (2)	COM FTC SBA	IEB	CO SB	CO SB	COM
Fraud. See Consumer protection, Inspectors General, White collar crime					
Free trade. See Trade agreements					
Freedom of information. See Government information, Privacy, Proprietary data					
Freight (2, 19)	TRA FMC ICC	FAA	TR	CO	COM TRA
Fringe benefits (6, 12)	LAB TRE OPM	PWBA IRS	EE GR	FI GA	LAB TRE
Fruits (1, 11)	AGR AGR	AMS FSIS	AG	AG	AGR
Fuel. See Coal, Natural gas, Petroleum					
Fugitives. See Extradition					
Funding gaps (9, 10)	TRE EOP	PDB OMB	AP WM	AP FI	TRE
Futures markets. See Commodity markets					
Gambling (14)	JUS JUS JUS	CRID EUSA FBI	JU	JU	COM
Gardening. See Horticulture					

	PARENTS	SUBUNITS	HOUSE	SENATE	FUNDING
Gas. See Natural gas					
Gasoline. See Petroleum					
Gems. See Precious stones					
Genealogy. See Federal records					
Genetics (17)	HHS HHS EOP OTA	NIAI NIGM STP	CO SC	CO LA	LAB
Genocide. See Human rights					
Geography. See Mapping					
Geology (16, 17)	INT NSF SI	GS	RE SC	CO EN	INT
Geothermal energy. See Energy research					
Gerontology. See Aged					
Global environment (8, 13, 17)	STA EOP NSF	OIE STP	CO SC	CO EP	COM VA
Gold. See Precious metals					
Government borrowing (9, 10)	TRE TRE TRE EOP	DFO FFB PDB NEC	WM	FI	TRE
Government contracts (10, 15)	DEF DEF LAB LAB EOP GAO GSA SBA	DCAA DLA ESA FECC OMB	BA EE GR NS SB	AR BA GA LA SB	DEF LAB
Government corporations (10)	EOP GAO	OMB	GR	GA	COM
Government employees (6, 10)	FLRA MSPB OPM SCO		GR	GA	TRE
Government ethics (10, 14)	GEO		GR, JU	GA, JU	TRE
Government fellowships (5)	EDU NFAH NSF SI	PE	EE	LA	LAB
Government information (3, 10)	JUS EOP GSA GSA LC NARA	IPO OMB IRMS ISO	GR JU	GA JU	COM TRE

	PARENTS	SUBUNITS	HOUSE	SENATE	FUNDING
Government liability (14)	JUS GAO	LCO	JU	JU	COM
Government litigation (14)	JUS JUS JUS	EUSA JSB SG	JU	JU	COM
Government loans. See Credit programs					
Government procurement (10)	DEF DEF EOP GSA	DLA REO FPP APO	GR NS	AR GA	DEF TRE
Government publications (3, 10)	COM GPO	NTIS	CO HO (JCP)	CO RU	LEG
Government securities (9, 10)	TRE TRE TRE FRB SEC	EPB PDB SBD	BA WM	BA FI	TRE
Government spending (9, 10)	TRE EOP EOP CBO GAO	FMS NEC OMB	AP BU GR	AP BU GA	TRE
Graduate education. See Government fellowships, Higher education, Student loans					
Grains (1)	AGR AGR AGR	AMS ASCS FGIS	AG	AG	AGR
Grand juries. See Criminal procedure					
Grazing lands (16)	INT	LMB	AG, RE	AG, EN	INT
Gross Domestic Product (2, 9)	COM EOP	EAB CEA	BA (JEC)	BA	COM
Ground transportation (2, 17, 19)	TRA ICC	FEHA	CO, SC, TR	CO EP	TRA
Guns. See Firearms					
Habeus corpus. See Court orders					
Handicapped (11, 12, 18)	EDU EDU EDU HHS SSA	NIDR RSA SERS DDA	CO EE SC WM	FI LA	LAB
Harbors (2, 4, 19)	COM TRA TRA FMC	NOAA CG MA	TR	CO EN EP	COM TRA
Hate crimes (14)	JUS JUS JUS	CRD FBI JSB	JU	JU	COM

	PARENTS	SUBUNITS	HOUSE	SENATE	FUNDING
Hazardous materials (8, 11)	LAB	OSHA	CO	CO	TRA
	TRA	FAA	TR	EP	VA
	TRA	FEHA			
	TRA	HMT			
	CPSC				
	EPA				
	NTSB				
Headaches. See Neuro- logical diseases					
Health care (11)	HHS	HCD	CO	LA	LAB
	HHS	HCPRA	VA	VA	VA
	HHS	HFB			
	HHS	HPB			
	HHS	MCHRD			
	VA	VHA			
	OTA				
Health data (11)	LAB	LSB	CO	LA	LAB
	HHS	NCHS			
	HHS	PHS			
Health education. See Preventive medicine					
Health food. See Nutrition					
Health insurance (9, 11)	HHS	HCFA	CO	FI	LAB
	CBO		GR	GA	TRE
	OPM		WM	LA	
Health maintenance organizations (11)	HHS	HCFA	CO	FI	LAB
	HHS	HMO	GR	GA	
	HHS	HRSA	WM	LA	
Hearing disorders (11)	HHS	NIDC	CO	LA	LAB
Heart disease (11)	HHS	NHL	CO	LA	LAB
Helicopters. See Aviation safety					
Herbicides (1, 8, 11)	AGR	ARS	AG	AG	AGR
	AGR	FS	CO	CO	VA
	HHS	FDA	SC	EP	
	EPA				
Hereditary diseases. See Genetics					
Heroin. See Drug abuse, Drug testing, Drug traffic					
High schools. See Secondary education					
Higher education (5)	EDU	PE	EE	LA	LAB
Highway construction (4, 19)	TRA	FEHA	TR	EP	TRA
Highway safety (11, 17, 19)	TRA	FEHA	CO	CO	TRA
	TRA	MCS	SC	EP	
	TRA	NHTSA	TR		
	NTSB				
Hijacking (14, 19)	JUS	FBI	JU	JU	COM
	TRA	CAS			TRA

	PARENTS	SUBUNITS	HOUSE	SENATE	FUNDING
Historic preservation (5, 16)	INT	NPS	BA	EN	INT
	GSA	PBS	HO	RU	
	NCPC		RE		
	PADC				
	SI				
Historical documents. See Federal records					
Holidays (10)	OPM		GR, JU	JU	TRE
Home building. See Housing industry					
Home economics (5)	AGR	ES	AG	AG	AGR
	EDU	VAE	EE	LA	LAB
Home entertainment. See Recording industry					
Home mortgages. See Mortgage loans					
Homelessness (12, 18, 20)	EDU	VAE	BA	BA	LAB
	HHS	CYFA	CO	FI	VA
	HHS	HRSA	EE	GA	
	HUD	CPD	GR	LA	
	HUD	MHP			
	FEMA				
	SSA				
Homesteading (20)	HUD	UHO	BA	BA	VA
	HUD	URO			
Horticulture (1)	AGR	APHIS	AG	AG	AGR
	AGR	NA			
	SI				
Hospice care. See Hospital facilities					
Hospital facilities (11)	HHS	HCPRA	CO	LA	LAB
	HHS	HRSA			
Hospital regulation (11, 18)	HHS	HCFA	CO	LA	LAB
	HHS	HRSA	VA	VA	VA
	VA	VHA			
House of Representatives. See Congressional organization					
Housing data. See Census					
Housing industry (9, 20)	HUD	CPD	BA	BA	VA
	HUD	PDR	(JEC)		
Housing management (12, 20)	HUD	FEHO	BA	BA	VA
	HUD	MHP			
Housing rehabilitation. See Construction industry, Mortgage loans, Public housing					
Human rights (13)	STA	HRHA	IR	FR	COM
	STA	IOA			FO
	SCEC				
Human subjects. See Medical research					

	PARENTS	SUBUNITS	HOUSE	SENATE	FUNDING
Humanitarian aid. See Foreign aid					
Humanities (5)	NFAH SI		EE HO	LA RU	INT
Hunger (13, 18)	AGR AGR IDCA	FAS FNS AID	AG EE IR	AG FR LA	AGR
Hunting. See Wildlife conservation					
Hurricanes. See Disaster relief					
Hydroelectric power (7, 8)	ENR INT	FERC RB	CO RE	EN	ENER
Identity papers (10, 14)	JUS TRE	INS SS	GR	GA	COM TRE
Illegal aliens. See Aliens					
Illiteracy. See Literacy					
Immigration (13, 14)	JUS JUS LAB STA	EOIR INS ILA CAB	JU	JU	COM
Immunization (11)	HHS	CDC	CO	LA	LAB
Impeachment (10, 14)	JUS JUS	AG CRID	JU	JU	COM LEG
Imports (2, 13)	COM COM STA TRE EOP ITC	FTZB IMP EBA CS TRO	CO IR WM	CO FI FR	COM
Impoundments (9, 10)	EOP GAO	OMB	AP RU	AP RU	TRE
Incinerators. See Waste management					
Income tax. See Taxation					
Indians (16, 18)	EDU HHS HHS HUD INT JUS LAB SI	INED IHS NAA IHO IAB LNR ETA	RE	IN	INT LAB
Indictments. See Criminal procedure					
Individual retirement accounts (9)	TRE	IRS	BA WM	BA FI	TRE
Indoor health (6, 11)	LAB EPA	OSHA	CO	LA	LAB

	PARENTS	SUBUNITS	HOUSE	SENATE	FUNDING
Industrial pollution (8, 11)	EOP EPA OTA	STP	CO	EN, EP	VA
Industrial relations. See Labor relations					
Industrial safety. See Occupational safety					
Industrial security (14, 15)	DEF ENR JUS	DIS SAO CRID	NS	JU	COM DEF
Industrial technology (2, 17)	COM COM COM EOP NSF OTA SBA	IEB NIST TPO STP	CO SB SC	CO SB (JEC)	COM VA
Infant mortality (11)	HHS	NICH	CO	LA	LAB
Infectious diseases. See Communicable diseases					
Inflation. See Economic data					
Influenza. See Communicable diseases					
Information management. See Federal paperwork, Govern ment information, Public administration					
Information resources. See Libraries					
Information science. See Computer technology					
Injunctions. See Judicial remedies					
Inland waterways (2, 4, 16, 19)	DEF INT TRA TRA ICC	ACE RD CG MA	RE TR	CO EN EP	COM TRA
Insects (1, 16)	AGR AGR AGR SI	APHIS ARS FS	AG	AG	AGR
Inspectors General (10)	EOP GAO	OMB	GR	GA	TRE
Insurance industry (2)	FRB FTC		BA CO	BA JU	COM
Insurance programs (4, 12, 20)	HUD VA FEMA IDCA SBA	FEHO VBA OPIC	BA SB VA	BA SB VA	VA

	PARENTS	SUBUNITS	HOUSE	SENATE	FUNDING
Intellectual property. See Copyrights					
Intelligence activities (13, 15)	DEF DEF DEF JUS JUS STA EOP	CCCI DIA IOO FBI IPR IRB CIA	IN IR JU NS	AR FR INT JU	DEF
Intelligence tests. See Education research					
Interagency relations (10)	EOP GAO	OMB	GR	GA	TRE
Interbranch relations. See Separation of powers					
Interest groups. See Lobbying					
Interest payments. See Taxation					
Interest rates (2, 9)	TRE TRE EOP FRB	DFO PDB NEC	BA WM (JEC)	BA FI	TRE VA
Intergovernmental relations (10, 20)	EOP ACIR GAO	OMB	GR	GA	TRE
Interjudicial relations. See Federal courts					
International agreements (13, 15)	STA STA STA STA STA STA	CAB EBA ECA IOA LAO PMA	IR	FR	COM
International arbitration (13)	STA USIP	FSE	IR	FR	COM
International boundaries (13)	STA STA	IRB LAO	IR	FR	COM
International claims (13, 14)	JUS STA	FCSC LAO	IR	FR	COM
International communication (2, 3, 13)	STA STA TRE FCC USIA	EBA ICIP CS	CO IR	CO FR	COM
International crime (13, 14)	JUS JUS STA STA	DEA INTER INM LEI	IR JU	FR JU	COM
International finance (9, 13)	COM STA TRE EOP EXIM FRB IDCA SEC	IEP IFD IAO NEC OPIC	BA IR WM	BA FI FR	COM FO

	PARENTS	SUBUNITS	HOUSE	SENATE	FUNDING
International law (13, 14)	JUS STA	LCO LAO	IR	FR	COM
International organizations (13)	STA TRE IDCA	IOA IAO	BA IR	BA FR	FO
International trade (2, 13)	AGR COM COM COM LAB STA TRA TRE EOP EOP FMC IDCA ITC SBA	FAS FTZB IEP ITA ILA EBA MA TIP NEC TRO TDA	AG BA CO IR SB WM (JEC)	AG BA CO FI FR SB	COM FO TRE
International transportation (2, 13, 19)	STA TRA FMC	EBA IAV	CO IR TR	CO EP FR	COM TRA
International travel (13)	COM STA USIA	TTA CAB	CO IR	CO FR	COM
International waters (13, 15)	DEF STA STA TRA	NAVY LAO OIE CG	IR	CO FR	COM
Internet. See Telecommunications					
Interstate commerce. See Congressional power					
Interstate relations (10, 14)	JUS	LSO	CO, JU	CO, JU	COM
Intervention abroad. See National security					
Inventions. See Patents					
Investment companies. See Securities industry					
Investment income. See Taxation					
Irrigation (1, 16)	AGR INT	SCS RB	AG RE	AG EN	AGR ENER

Job training. See Apprentice-
  ship, Vocational rehabilita-
  tion, Welfare					

Journalistic confidentiality (3, 14)	JUS JUS	CID LCO	JU	JU	COM
Judicial administration (10, 14)	JUS	JMD	JU	JU	COM
Judicial circuits. See Federal courts					

	PARENTS	SUBUNITS	HOUSE	SENATE	FUNDING
Judicial ethics (14)	JUS	AG	JU	JU	COM
Judicial power. See Federal courts					
Judicial punishment. See Sentences					
Judicial remedies (14)	JUS JUS	PDO SG	JU	JU	COM
Juries (14)	JUS JUS	EUSA PDO	JU	JU	COM
Juvenile delinquency (5, 14)	EDU HHS JUS JUS	CEP CYFA JJDP NIJ	EE JU	JU LA	COM LAB
Labor markets (6)	LAB	ETA	EE (JEC)	LA	LAB
Labor relations (6)	LAB FLRA FMCS NLRB NMB OPM	LMR	EE GR (JEC)	GA LA	LAB TRE
Labor standards (6)	LAB LAB	ESA LMS	EE	LA	LAB
Laboratory research (17)	COM NSF OTA	NIST	SC	CO	COM
Lakes. See Inland waterways					
Land management (1, 16)	AGR AGR HUD INT INT TVA	FS SCS EEO LMB NPS	AG BA	AG BA	INT
Land sales (2, 4, 20)	HUD FTC	ILS	BA	BA	VA
Landfills. See Waste management					
Languages. See Humanities					
Law enforcement (14)	JUS JUS JUS JUS JUS TRE TRE TRE TRE TRE	EUSA FBI INS MS NIJ ATF CS FLET IRS SS	JU	JU	COM TRE
Laws of war. See International law, Martial law, Neutrality law					

	PARENTS	SUBUNITS	HOUSE	SENATE	FUNDING
Learning disabilities (5, 18)	EDU HHS HHS	SERS DDA NICH	EE CO	LA	LAB
Legal immunity. See Diplomatic immunity, Foreign sovereign immunity, Government liability					
Legal opinions (10, 14)	JUS STA GAO MSPB	LCO LAO	GR JU	GA JU	COM TRE
Legal services (14)	LSC		JU	LA	COM
Legal tender. See Currency					
Legislative delegation. See Administrative law					
Legislative investigations. See Congressional power					
Legislative leaders. See Congressional organization					
Legislative process. See Congressional operations					
Lending. See Credit programs, Financial institutions, Interest rates					
Liability insurance. See Product liability					
Libraries (5)	EDU GPO LC NCLIS NFAH	LPD	EE HO	LA RU	LAB LEG
Lie detectors. See Polygraphs					
Life insurance. See Insurance industry					
Life sciences. See Biotechnology, Genetics, Medical research					
Liquor. See Alcoholic beverages					
Literacy (5)	EDU EDU EDU EDU EDU ACTION	CEP ERI NIE NIL VAE VISTA	EE	LA	LAB
Literature. See Humanities					
Livestock (1)	AGR AGR AGR	AMS APHIS PSA	AG	AG	AGR

	PARENTS	SUBUNITS	HOUSE	SENATE	FUNDING
Lobbying (10, 14)	JUS TRE	CRID IRS	HO, JU, WM	FI, GA, RU	COM TRE
Local governments (9, 10,20)	COM TRE ACIR	CB RSO	GR	GA	COM TRE
Lockouts. See Labor relations					
Long-term care. See Nursing homes					
Lotteries (2, 10)	JUS PS	CRID	GR JU	GA JU	COM
Magazines. See Copyrights					
Magistrates. See Federal judges					
Mail delivery. See Postal Service					
Mail order sales. See Consumer protection					
Manufacturing. See Economic data					
Mapping (10, 16)	COM COM DEF INT EOP	CB NOAA DMA GS CIA	CO NS RE	AR CO EP	COM DEF INT
Marihuana. See Drug abuse, Drug testing, Drug traffic					
Marine Corps (15)	DEF	NAVY	NS	AR	DEF
Marine resources (8, 16, 17)	COM INT STA EOP OTA	NOAA FWS OIE STP	RE SC	CO EP	COM INT
Marine safety (6, 11, 19)	LAB TRA NTSB	OSHA CG	TR	CO	TRA
Maritime industry (2, 13, 16)	STA TRA TRA FMC	EBA CG MA	TR	CO	COM TRA
Martial law (13, 15)	DEF STA EOP	JCS PMA NSC	IR NS	AR FR	DEF
Mass media. See Broadcasting					
Mass transit (19, 20)	TRA NTSB	FTA	TR	BA	TRA
Meat (1, 11)	AGR AGR AGR	AMS FSIS PSA	AG	AG	AGR
Medal of Freedom (10)	EOP	WHO	GR	GA	TRE
Medal of Honor (15)	DEF	SOD	NS	AR	DEF

	PARENTS	SUBUNITS	HOUSE	SENATE	FUNDING
Medicaid. See Health insurance					
Medical devices (11, 17)	HHS	FDA	CO	LA	AGR
Medical insurance. See Health insurance					
Medical laboratories (2, 11)	HHS	FDA	CO	LA	LAB
Medical malpractice. See Health insurance					
Medical research (11, 17)	HHS HHS HHS	HCPRA NIH NLM	CO SC	LA	LAB
Medical tests. See Health care					
Medicare. See Health insurance					
Medication. See Drug safety					
Members of Congress (10)	JUS JUS	CID CRID	HO ST	ET RU	LEG
Memory loss. See Neurological diseases					
Mental health (11)	HHS	NIMH	CO	LA	LAB
Mental illness. See Handicapped					
Merchant marine. See Maritime industry					
Metals. See Mining industry					
Meteorology. See Weather					
Metric system. See Weights and measures					
Metropolitan areas. See Local governments					
Migrant workers (6, 18)	EDU HHS LAB LAB	CEP HRSA ESA ETA	EE	LA	LAB
Migration. See Census					
Military assistance (13, 15)	DEF DEF STA EOP	DSA ISA PMA NSC	IR NS	AR FR	DEF FO
Military education. See Service academies					
Military installations (4, 15)	DEF	INST	NS	AR	MC
Military law (15)	DEF	JAG	NS	AR	DEF
Military operations (15)	DEF DEF	CCCI JCS	NS	AR	DEF

	PARENTS	SUBUNITS	HOUSE	SENATE	FUNDING
Military personnel (15)	DEF	FMP	NS	AR	DEF
Military research (15, 17)	DEF	ARPA	NS	AR	DEF
	DEF	DLA			
	DEF	REO			
	OTA				

Military reserves. See
  National Guard

Military sales. See
  Arms exports

Military strategy. See
  National security

Milk. See Dairy industry

	PARENTS	SUBUNITS	HOUSE	SENATE	FUNDING
Mine safety (6, 11)	INT	MB	EE	LA	INT
	LAB	MSHA			LAB
	FMSH				
Mineral leases (2, 7, 16)	COM	NOAA	RE	EN	COM
	INT	LMB			INT
	INT	MMS			
Mineral resources (8, 16)	INT	GS	RE	EN	INT
	INT	LMB	SC		
	INT	MB			
	INT	MMS			
	STA	OIE			
	EOP	STP			
	OTA				

Minimum wage. See Wages

	PARENTS	SUBUNITS	HOUSE	SENATE	FUNDING
Mining industry (2, 8)	INT	MB	CO	EN	INT
	INT	SMRE	RE		VA
	EPA				

Minorities. See Ethnic groups

Missiles. See Weapons

	PARENTS	SUBUNITS	HOUSE	SENATE	FUNDING
Missing children (18)	HHS	CYFA	EE	JU	LAB
	HHS	FYS	JU	LA	
	JUS	FBI			
	JUS	JJDP			
Mobile homes (11, 19)	HUD	MHS	CO	CO	VA
	TRA	NHTSA	TR		

Monetary policy. See Government securities, Interest
  rates, Money supply

Money. See Currency

	PARENTS	SUBUNITS	HOUSE	SENATE	FUNDING
Money laundering (9, 14)	JUS	DEA	BA	BA	COM
	TRE	IRS			TRE
	FDIC				
	FRB				

Money orders. See
  Negotiable instruments

	PARENTS	SUBUNITS	HOUSE	SENATE	FUNDING
Money supply (9, 10)	TRE	MAO	BA	BA	TRE
	FRB				

Monopolies. See Antitrust law

	PARENTS	SUBUNITS	HOUSE	SENATE	FUNDING
Monuments (5)	INT FAC NCPC	NPS	HO RE	EN RU	INT
Mortality rates. See Health data					
Mortgage loans (9, 20)	HUD HUD HUD	FEHO MHP SHP	BA VA	BA VA	VA

Mortgage securities. See
  Government securities,
  Interest rates,
  Securities industry					

Most Favored Nation Status. See Trade agreements					

Motor vehicles. See Automobile
  industry, Ground transporta-
  tion, Highway safety					

Moving industry (2, 19)	ICC		CO	CO	TRA
Multinational corporations (2, 9, 13)	COM STA TRE TRE TRE EOP	ITA EBA CC IRS TIP TRO	IR WM (JEC)	FI FR	COM TRE
Municipal and state bonds. See Securities industry					
Municipalities. See Local governments					
Munitions. See Weapons					
Museums (5)	NFAH SI		EE HO	LA RU	INT
Mutual funds. See Securities industry					
Narcotics. See Drug abuse, Drug testing, Drug traffic					
National banks. See Bank regulation					

National borders. See
  Airspace, Border patrol,
  Territorial waters					

National debt. See Public debt					
National emergencies. See Presidency					
National Guard (15)	DEF	NGB	NS	AR	DEF
National landmarks. See Historic preservation					

National libraries. See Agri-
  cultural research, Libraries,
  Medical research					

	PARENTS	SUBUNITS	HOUSE	SENATE	FUNDING
National security (13, 15)	DEF	DIS	IR	AR	COM
	DEF	ISP	NS	FR	DEF
	DEF	JCS			
	DEF	NSA			
	ENR	IAE			
	JUS	IPR			
	STA	PMA			
	EOP	NSC			
	OTA				

National wealth. See
  Gross Domestic Product

Native Americans. See Indians

Natural disasters. See
  Disaster relief

Natural gas (7, 16)	ENR	ERA	CO	CO	INT
	ENR	FEO	SC	EN	
	INT	MMS			

Naturalization (10, 14)	JUS	INS	JU	JU	COM

Navy. See Armed forces

Neglect of duty. See
  Inspectors General

Negotiable instruments (2, 9)	FDIC		BA	BA	COM
	FRB		CO		TRE
	SEC				

Neurological diseases (11)	HHS	NIND	CO	LA	LAB

Neutrality law (13, 14)	COM	ITA	IR	FR	COM
	JUS	CRID			
	STA	EBA			
	STA	LAO			
	TRE	CS			

Newspapers. See Journal-
  istic confidentiality

Noise pollution (8, 17)	LAB	OSHA	CO	CO	VA
	EPA		SC	EP	

Nominations. See Presidency

Nonprofit organizations (3, 5)	TRE	IRS	WM	FI	TRE
	NFAH				
	PS				

North Atlantic Treaty Organization (NATO) (13, 15)	DEF	ISP	IR	FR	DEF
	STA	EUR			COM
	EOP	NSC			

Nuclear deterrence. See
  Military research, National
  security, Weapons

Nuclear energy (7, 16, 17)	ENR	DPO	CO	AR	ENER
	ENR	ERA	NS	EN	
	ENR	FERC	RE	EP	
	ENR	NEO	SC	GA	
	EOP	STP			
	OTA				

Nuclear facilities (7, 8)	ENR	ESH	CO	EP	ENER
	NRC		RE	GA	

	PARENTS	SUBUNITS	HOUSE	SENATE	FUNDING
Nuclear proliferation (13, 15)	DEF ENR STA EOP ACDA	ISP INN OIE NSC	IR NS	AR FR GA	COM DEF
Nuclear safety (8, 11)	ENR FEMA NRC	ESH	CO RE	EN	ENER
Nuclear testing (15, 17)	DEF ENR ACDA	DNA DPO	IR NS	AR FR	DEF ENER
Nuclear waste (8, 17)	ENR ENR ENR ENR EOP NRC OTA	CRW DPO NEO RAW STP	CO RE SC	EN EP GA	ENER
Numismatics (2, 5)	TRE	MINT	BA	BA	TRE
Nursing homes (11, 18)	HHS HUD VA	HCFA MHP VHA	BA, CO, VA, WM	BA, FI, LA, VA	LAB VA
Nutrition (5, 11)	AGR AGR HHS HHS	FNS IINIS FDA NIDD	AG CO	AG LA	AGR
Obesity. See Eating disorders					
Obscenity (3, 14)	JUS FCC PS	CRID	JU	JU	COM
Obstruction of justice (14)	JUS JUS	CRID EUSA	JU	JU	COM
Occupational safety (6, 11)	HHS LAB OSHR	NIOS OSHA	EE GR SB	GA LA SB	LAB
Ocean policy (8, 13, 16, 19)	COM DEF STA TRA	NOAA ISA OIE MA	IR SC TR	CO EP FR	COM DEF
Oceanography (8, 16, 17)	COM DEF TRA NOF OTA	NOAA NRO CG	RE CO	CO	COM DEF
Official misconduct. See Corrupt practices.					
Offshore drilling (7, 17)	COM ENR INT NSF	NOAA FERC MMS	CO RE SC	CO EN	ENER INT
Oil. See Petroleum					
Oil spills (8, 19)	TRA EPA NTSB	CG	CO TR	CO EP	TRA VA
Olympic games. See Sports					

	PARENTS	SUBUNITS	HOUSE	SENATE	FUNDING
Open market operations. See Money supply					
Opiates. See Drug abuse, Drug safety, Medical research					
Organ transplants (11, 17)	HHS HHS	HRSA NIAI	CO	LA	LAB
Organized crime (14)	JUS JUS JUS	CRID EUSA FBI	JU	GA JU	COM
Orphans. See Family services					
Orthopedics (11)	HHS	NIAM	CO	LA	LAB
Outdoor recreation See Recreation areas					
Outer continental shelf (7, 16)	INT INT	GS MMS	RE	CO EN	INT
Overseas business. See Exports, Multinational corporations, Tariffs					
Overseas conflicts. See Military assistance, Neutrality law, War powers					
Overseas mail. See Customs					
Overseas posts. See Armed forces, Diplomatic service, Foreign aid					
Ozone layer. See Atmosphere					
Panama Canal (2, 13, 15)	STA PCC	IAA	NS	AR CO	COM TRA
Paralysis. See Neurological diseases					
Pardons (14)	JUS EOP	PAO WHO	JU	JU	COM
Parks. See Recreation areas					
Parole (14)	JUS	PC	JU	JU	COM
Partisan activities. See Government employees					
Partnerships. See Taxation					
Passenger ships (2, 19)	TRA FMC NTSB	CG	TR	CO	COM TRA
Passports. See International travel					
Patents (14, 17)	COM STA ITC	PTO EBA	JU SC	CO JU	COM

	PARENTS	SUBUNITS	HOUSE	SENATE	FUNDING
Payroll taxes. See Taxation					
Peacekeeping forces. See International organizations, Military assistance, National security					
Pediatrics. See Child health					
Pensions (6, 9, 10, 12)	LAB TRE VA CBO OPM PBGC	PWBA IRS VBA	EE GR VA	GA LA VA	LAB TRE VA
Performing arts. See Arts					
Personal data. See Privacy					
Personal finance. See Bank deposits, Consumer credit, Individual retirement accounts, Insurance industry, Pensions, Securities industry					
Pesticides (1, 8, 11)	AGR HHS EPA	ARS FDA	AG CO	AG LA	AGR VA
Petroleum (7, 8, 16)	ENR ENR INT	FEO FERC MMS	CO RE SC	EN	ENER INT
Pharmaceutical industry. See Drug safety					
Philanthropy. See Charitable organizations					
Philately (2, 5)	TRE PS	EPB	GR	GA	TRE
Phobias. See Mental health					
Physical disability. See Handicapped					
Physical education (5, 11)	HHS	PHS	CO	LA	LAB
Physical security (10)	INT TRE GSA PS	NPS SS PBS	GR HO	GA RU	TRE
Pipelines (2, 7, 8, 17)	ENR ENR TRA NTSB	ERA FERC PSO	CO RE TR	CO EN	ENER TRA
Piracy. See International crime					
Plants (1, 16)	AGR AGR AGR SI	APHIS ARS NA	AG	AG	AGR

	PARENTS	SUBUNITS	HOUSE	SENATE	FUNDING
Plastics (2, 17)	COM CPSC NSF	NIST	CO SC	CO	COM VA
Plea bargaining. _See_ Criminal procedure					
Poisons. _See_ Toxic substances					
Polar regions (13, 17)	STA TRA NSF	OIE CG	IR SC	CO FR	COM VA
Police forces. _See_ Law enforcement, Military law, Physical security					
Police misconduct (14)	JUS JUS	CRD FBI	JU	JU	COM
Policy implementation. _See_ Executive branch operations, Interagency relations, Intergovernmental relations					
Political asylum (10, 13)	JUS STA	INS HRHA	IR JU	FR JU	COM
Political expression. _See_ Broadcasting, Lobbying, Public demonstrations					
Political fundraising. _See_ Elections					
Political liaison. _See_ Congressional-executive relations					
Political parties. See Congressional organization, Elections, Members of Congress					
Pollution. _See_ Acid rain, Air pollution, Industrial pollution, Noise pollution, Waste management, Water pollution					
Polygraphs (6, 14)	DEF JUS JUS LAB OPM OTA	DIS PDO NIJ ESA	EE GR JU	GA JU LA	COM LAB TRE
Population data. _See_ Census					
Population growth (8, 11, 13)	COM HHS STA IDCA	CB NICH OIE AID	CO IR	FR LA	FO LAB
Pornography (14)	JUS PS	CRID	JU	JU	COM
Ports. _See_ Harbors					
Postal Service (2, 3, 10)	PRC PS		GR	GA	TRE

	PARENTS	SUBUNITS	HOUSE	SENATE	FUNDING
Poultry (1)	AGR	AMS	AG	AG	AGR
	AGR	APHIS			
	AGR	FSIS			
	AGR	PSA			
Poverty level. See Census					
Poverty programs. See Food stamps, Homelessness, Welfare					
Power plants. See Electric power					
Precious metals (2, 9, 16)	INT	MB	BA	BA	INT
	TRE	MINT			TRE
	CFTC				
	FRB				
Precious stones (2, 16)	COM	ITA	CO	CO	COM
	INT	MB	WM	FI	INT
	ITC				
	SI				
Prenatal care (11, 18)	HHS	NICH	CO	LA	LAB
	HHS	PHS			
Preschool education (5)	EDU	ESE	EE	LA	LAB
	HHS	CHB			
Prescription drugs. See Drug safety, Health insurance, Product labeling					
Presidency (10)	JUS	AG	GR	GA	COM
	TRE	SS	HO	JU	TRE
	EOP	WHO	JU	RU	
	FEC				
	LC	CRS			
	NARA				
Presidential-congressional relations. See Congressional-executive relations					
Pretrial procedure. See Civil procedure, Criminal procedure, Trials					
Preventive medicine (5, 11)	HHS	CDC	CO	LA	LAB
	HHS	HCPRA			
	HHS	NIH			
Price controls. See Economic controls					
Price supports. See Agricultural subsidies					
Prices. See Consumer Price Index					
Prisoners (14)	JUS	JAB	JU	JU	COM
	JUS	MS			
	JUS	NIJ			
	JUS	PB			
	JUS	PC			
Prisons. See Correctional facilities					

	PARENTS	SUBUNITS	HOUSE	SENATE	FUNDING
Privacy (3, 14, 17)	DEF JUS EOP EOP NARA OTA	DPB IPO OMB STP	GR JU SC	CO GA JU	COM TRE
Private litigation. See Civil procedure					
Private property. See Eminent domain					
Private schools (5)	EDU EDU EDU	ESE PE PRE	EE	LA	LAB
Probation. See Sentences					
Proclamations. See Executive orders					
Product labeling (2, 11)	HHS TRE CPSC FTC	FDA ATF	CO	CO	COM VA
Product liability (2, 14)	JUS CPSC	CID	CO JU	CO JU	COM VA
Product safety (11, 17)	COM HHS CPSC FTC	NIST FDA	CO	CO	COM VA
Product tampering (11, 14)	AGR HHS JUS	FSIS FDA FBI	CO JU	JU LA	AGR COM
Productivity. See Economic data					
Program review. See Congressional oversight					
Property insurance. See Insurance industry					
Property rights. See Copy- rights, Patents, Trademarks					
Proprietary data (2, 3)	ENR JUS FTC SEC	FERC IPO	CO	CO	COM ENER
Prosthetic standards. See Medical devices					
Psychological disorders. See Mental health					
Public administration (10)	EOP ACUS GAO GSA NARA OPM	OMB	GR	GA	TRE

	PARENTS	SUBUNITS	HOUSE	SENATE	FUNDING
Public broadcasting (3, 5)	COM FCC NFAH	NTIA	CO	CO	COM
Public buildings (4, 10)	FAC GSA NCPC NFAH	PBS	TR	EP GA	INT TRE
Public debt (9, 10)	TRE TRE EOP EOP CBO	FFB PDB NEC OMB	BU WM (JEC)	BU FI	TRE

Public defenders.
  See Legal services

	PARENTS	SUBUNITS	HOUSE	SENATE	FUNDING
Public demonstrations (3, 14)	INT JUS	NPS MS	JU	JU	COM INT

Public finance. See Budget
  deficits, Budget formulation, Government borrowing,
  Government spending, Public
  debt, Taxation

	PARENTS	SUBUNITS	HOUSE	SENATE	FUNDING
Public housing (4, 20)	HUD	PHO	BA	BA	VA
Public lands (8, 16)	AGR INT INT JUS	FS LMB NPS LNR	RE	EN	INT

Public officials. See
  Congressional employees,
  Diplomatic service, Federal
  judges, Government employees,
  Members of Congress, Military
  personnel

	PARENTS	SUBUNITS	HOUSE	SENATE	FUNDING
Public schools (5)	EDU EDU	ESE PE	EE	LA	LAB

Public transportation.
  See Mass transit

	PARENTS	SUBUNITS	HOUSE	SENATE	FUNDING
Public utilities (7, 8)	ENR NRC TVA	FERC	CO RE TR	EN EP	ENER

Publications. See Copyrights,
  Government publications,
  Libraries

Purchasing power. See
  Consumer Price Index

Quotas. See Agricultural
  production, Immigration,
  Imports

Racketeering. See
  Organized crime

	PARENTS	SUBUNITS	HOUSE	SENATE	FUNDING
Radiation (6, 8, 11, 17)	COM	NIST	CO	CO	ENER
	ENR	ESH	EE	EP	LAB
	HHS	FDA	RE	LA	VA
	LAB	OSHA	SC		
	EOP	STP			
	EPA				
	FEMA				
	NRC				
	OTA				

Radio industry. See
  Broadcasting

Radioactive waste. See
  Nuclear waste

Radioactivity. See
  Nuclear safety

	PARENTS	SUBUNITS	HOUSE	SENATE	FUNDING
Radon (8, 11)	EPA		CO	EP	VA
Railroad industry (2, 19)	TRA	FRA	TR	CO	TRA
	ICC				
Railroad safety (11, 17, 19)	TRA	FRA	TR	CO	TRA
	NTSB				

Rainfall. See Flood control,
  Water supply, Weather

	PARENTS	SUBUNITS	HOUSE	SENATE	FUNDING
Real estate industry (4, 9, 20)	HUD	FEHO	BA	BA	VA
	TRE	IRS	WM (JEC)	FI	

Recalls. See Product safety

Recession. See Economic data

Reclamation. See
  Land management

	PARENTS	SUBUNITS	HOUSE	SENATE	FUNDING
Recording industry (2, 3, 14, 17)	FCC		CO	CO	COM
			JU	JU	

Records management. See
  Federal paperwork

	PARENTS	SUBUNITS	HOUSE	SENATE	FUNDING
Recreation areas (8, 16)	AGR	FS	RE	EN	INT
	INT	FWS			
	INT	LMB			
	INT	NPS			
	INT	RB			
	TVA				

Recycling. See
  Waste management

Red tape. See
  Federal paperwork

	PARENTS	SUBUNITS	HOUSE	SENATE	FUNDING
Refugees (13, 14, 18)	HHS	RRO	EE	FR	COM
	JUS	CORS	IR	JU	LAB
	JUS	INS	JU	LA	
	STA	IOA			
	STA	RPB			

Regulatory procedure.
  See Administrative law

	PARENTS	SUBUNITS	HOUSE	SENATE	FUNDING
Rehabilitation services (5, 11, 18)	EDU EDU HHS VA	RSA SERS DDA VHA	CO EE VA	LA VA	LAB VA
Religious institutions (3, 18)	JUS TRE	CID IRS	JU WM	FI JU	COM
Remedial instruction. See Compensatory education					
Renewable energy. See Energy conservation					
Rent control. See Economic controls					
Rental housing. See Housing management					
Repatriation (13)	STA	RPB	IR	FR	COM
Representation. See Congressional districts, Elections, Voting					
Representatives. See Members of Congress					
Rescue services (19)	TRA TRA	ETO CG	TR	CO	TRA
Reservoirs. See Water supply					
Resource shortages (2, 7, 13, 16)	COM ENR INT TRE	ITA IAE MB TIP	CO RE	CO EN	COM ENER
Respiratory diseases (11)	HHS HHS	NHL NIAI	CO	EP LA	LAB
Restitution. See Crime victims, Government contracts, Judicial remedies					
Retail trade. See Economic data					
Retirement (6, 12, 18)	LAB TRE OPM SSA	PWBA IRS	EE GR WM	FI GA LA	LAB TRE
Revenue. See Taxation					
Revenue sharing (9, 10)	COM TRE	CB RSO	GR WM	FI GA	TRE
Rights-of-way (8, 19)	INT TRA TRA	LMB FEHA FRA	RE	EN	INT TRA
Riots. See Civil disorders					
Rivers. See Inland waterways					

	PARENTS	SUBUNITS	HOUSE	SENATE	FUNDING
Roads. *See* Highway construction					
Robotics. *See* Industrial technology					
Royalties. *See* Copyrights, Mineral leases, Patents					
Runaways. *See* Missing children					
Rural areas (1, 2, 4)	AGR AGR AGR AGR SBA	ES FAHA RDA REA	AG SB	AG SB	AGR
Sabotage. *See* Subversive activities					
Saline water. *See* Water supply					
Salt. *See* Nutrition					
Salvage (13, 14)	JUS STA TRA	CID LAO CG	IR TR	CO FR	COM
Sanitation. *See* Waste management					
Satellites. *See* Space communication					
Savings and loan associations. *See* Financial institutions					
Savings bonds. *See* Government securities					
Scholarships. *See* Government fellowships					
Scientific research. *See* Agricultural research, Energy research, Environmental research, Laboratory research, Medical research, Military research					
Seabed mining. *See* Undersea exploration					
Seal of the U.S. (10, 14)	STA	SOS	JU	JU	COM
Searches and seizures. *See* Law enforcement					
Seashores. *See* Recreation areas					
Secondary education (5)	EDU	ESE	EE	LA	LAB
Securities industry (2, 9)	TRE FRB SEC	FIP	BA CO	BA	COM TRE
Sedatives. *See* Drug safety					

	PARENTS	SUBUNITS	HOUSE	SENATE	FUNDING
Seeds. See Agricultural research, Horticulture, Plants					
Selective Service (15)	SSS		NS	AR	VA
Self-employment. See Taxation					
Senate. See Congressional organization					
Senators. See Members of Congress					
Senior citizens. See Aged					
Sentences (14)	JUS	SC	JU	JU	COM
Separation of powers (10, 14)	JUS	AG	GR	GA	COM
	LC	CRS	JU	JU	LEG
Service academies (5, 15)	DEF	AF	NS	AR	DEF
	DEF	ARMY	TR	CO	TRA
	DEF	NAVY			
	TRA	CG			
	TRA	MA			
Sewage treatment. See Waste management					
Shipping. See Freight, Maritime industry, Water transportation					
Shoreline erosion. See Coastal zone management					
Shoreline patrol. See Territorial waters					
Silver. See Precious metals					
Skin diseases (11)	HHS	NIAM	CO	LA	LAB
Sleep disorders. See Mental health					
Slum clearance (20)	HUD	PDR	BA	BA	VA
	HUD	UDAG			
Small business (2, 4, 20)	COM	MBDA	SB	SB	COM
	FEMA			(JEC)	
	GSA	SBD			
	SBA				
Smog. See Air pollution					
Smoking (11)	HHS	NCI	CO	LA	LAB
	HHS	NHL			
	HHS	SHO			
	FTC				
Smuggling (14)	JUS	DEA	IR	FR	COM
	JUS	INS	JU	JU	TRE
	TRA	CG			
	TRA	FAA			
	TRE	CS			

	PARENTS	SUBUNITS	HOUSE	SENATE	FUNDING
State power. See Congressional power, Intergovernmental relations, Interstate relations					
Statistical data. See Census, Crime data, Economic data, Education data, Energy data, Health data					
Statutory interpretation. See Federal courts					
Stock markets. See Securities industry					
Storms. See Disaster relief, Insurance industry, Weather					
Strategic stockpiles (15, 16)	COM DEF ENR STA FEMA GSA OTA	SRO DLA DPO EBA FPR	NS 3C	AR	COM DEF
Strikes. See Labor relations					
Stroke. See Neurological diseases					
Student loans (5, 9)	EDU HHS	PE HPB	EE	LA	LAB
Students. See Education data					
Subsidies. See Business assistance, Credit programs, Insurance programs					
Subsidized housing. See Housing management, Mortgage loans, Public housing					
Subversive activities (14, 15)	JUS JUS JUS	CRID FBI INTER	JU	JU	COM
Subways. See Mass transit					
Sugar (1, 11)	AGR AGR HHS CFTC	ASCS HNIS FDA	AG	AG	AGR
Suicide. See Mental health					
Supreme Court. See Federal courts					
Surplus property. See Federal property					
Survivor benefits (12, 18)	VA OPM SSA	VBA	CO GR VA	GA LA VA	LAB TRE VA
Synthetic fuels. See Energy research					

	PARENTS	SUBUNITS	HOUSE	SENATE	FUNDING
Tape recordings. See Recording industry					
Tariffs (2, 9, 13)	COM TRE EOP EOP ITC	IMP CS NEC TRO	WM (JEC)	FI	COM TRE
Tax evasion. See Taxation					
Tax expenditures. See Taxation					
Taxation (9, 10)	TRE TRE EOP EOP CBO	IRS TPO CEA NEC	BU WM (JEC)	BU FI	TRE
Technological risk (17)	EOP NSF OTA	STP	SC	CO	VA
Technology transfer (2, 8, 13, 17)	COM COM DEF STA TRE TRE EPA	EXP TPO DTSA OIE CS TIP	CO SC	CO	COM DEF
Telecommunications (2, 3, 17)	COM DEF DEF STA EOP FCC OTA	NTIA CCCI DCA ICIP STP	CO NS SC	AR CO	COM
Telemarketing. See Consumer protection					
Telephone service. See Telecommunications					
Television industry. See Broadcasting					
Tenants. See Housing Management					
Territorial waters (8, 15)	COM JUS TRA	NOAA LNR CG	RE TR	CO	COM TRA
Territories (10)	INT STA	TIA PIA	JU RE	EN JU	COM INT
Terrorism (13, 14, 15)	DEF JUS JUS STA STA EOP	SOO FBI INTER DSB SOS NSC	IR JU	FR JU	COM
Thrift industry. See Financial institutions					

	PARENTS	SUBUNITS	HOUSE	SENATE	FUNDING
Tidelands. See Coastal zone management					
Timber resources (8, 16)	AGR INT	FS LMB	AG RE	AG EN	INT
Time zones (19)	TRA	SOT	CO	CO	TRA
Tobacco industry (1, 14)	AGR AGR TRE TRE	AMS ASCS ATF IRS	AG CO WM	AG CO FI	AGR TRE
Topography. See Mapping.					
Tornadoes. See Disaster relief					
Torts. See Civil procedure					
Tourism (2)	COM	TTA	CO	CO	COM
Toxic substances (8, 11)	HHS HHS HHS LAB CPSC EPA	FDA NIEH TSDR OSHA	CO SC	EP LA	LAB VA
Toys. See Product safety					
Trade agreements (2, 13)	COM STA EOP ITC	ITA EBA TRO	WM	FI	COM TRE
Trade deficits (2, 13)	COM STA TRE EOP	EAB EBA IAO NEC	CO WM (JEC)	CO FI	COM
Trade disputes and remedies. See Trade agreements					
Trade secrets. See Proprietary data					
Trademarks (2, 14)	COM STA	PTO EBA	JU	JU	COM
Traffic accidents. See Highway safety					
Trains. See Railroad industry					
Trash. See Waste management					
Trauma (11)	HHS	NIGM	CO	LA	LAB
Travel industry. See Tourism					
Treason (13, 14)	JUS	FBI	JU	JU	COM
Treasury securities. See Government securities					
Treaties (13, 14, 15)	JUS STA STA	LCO LAO TAO	IR	FR	COM

	PARENTS	SUBUNITS	HOUSE	SENATE	FUNDING
Trees. See Forestry					
Trials (14)	JUS JUS	EUSA PDO	JU	JU	COM
Tribal rights. See Indians					
Trucking industry (2, 19)	ICC		CO, TR	CO	TRA
Trust funds (9, 12)	TRE EOP CBO SSA	FMS NEC	BU WM	BU FI	TRE
Tuition. See Student loans					
Tunnels (4, 19)	TRA TRA	FEHA FRA	TR	EP	TRA
Underground exploration (7, 16, 17)	ENR INT EOP OTA	FEO MB STP	RE SC	CO EN	ENER INT
Undersea exploration (16, 17)	COM DEF STA EOP NSF OTA	NOAA NRO OIE STP	RE	CO EN	COM VA
Unemployment compensation (6, 12)	LAB	ETA	WM	FI	LAB
Unemployment rate (6)	LAB	LSB	EE (JEC)	LA	LAB
Unions. See Labor relations					
United Nations. See International organizations					
Universities. See Higher education					
Uranium. See Nuclear energy					
Utility rates. See Energy prices, Public utilities, Telecommunications					
Vacations. See Tourism					
Vaccination. See Immunization					
Vegetables. See Fruits					
Venereal disease (11)	HHS HHS	CDC NIAI	CO	LA	LAB
Veterans (5, 6, 11, 12)	EDU LAB VA VA OPM SBA	VPO VETS VBA VHA	VA	VA	LAB VA
Veterinary medicine. See Animals					

	PARENTS	SUBUNITS	HOUSE	SENATE	FUNDING
Veto power. See Congressional-executive relations					
Vice-Presidency. See Presidency					
Victim assistance. See Crime victims, Disaster relief, Workers compensation					
Video equipment. See Recording industry					
Violent crime (14)	JUS JUS JUS JUS	EUSA FBI JAB NIJ	JU	JU	COM
Viruses. See Communicable diseases					
Visas. See International travel					
Visual arts. See Arts					
Visual disorders (11)	EDU HHS SSA	SERS NEI	CO	LA	LAB
Vital records. See Privacy					
Vitamins. See Nutrition					
Vocational education (5, 6)	EDU VA	VAE VBA	EE VA	LA VA	LAB VA
Vocational rehabilitation (6, 18)	EDU LAB VA EEOC	SERS ETA VBA	CO EE VA	LA VA	LAB VA
Volcanoes. See Geology					
Volunteer services (5, 18)	VA ACTION NCSC PCO	VHA VISTA	EE IR	FR LA	FO LAB VA
Voting (10, 14)	JUS CRC	CRD	JU	JU	COM
Wage controls. See Economic controls					
Wages (6)	DEF LAB LAB LAB EEOC OPM	FMP ESA LSD WIR	EE GR NS (JEC)	AR GA LA	LAB TRE
War powers (10, 13, 14)	JUS EOP LC	AG NSC CRS	IR	FR	COM LEG
Warfare (13, 15)	DEF STA EOP	ISP PMA NSC	IR NS	AR FR	COM DEF

	PARENTS	SUBUNITS	HOUSE	SENATE	FUNDING
Warranties. See Consumer protection					
Washington, D.C. See District of Columbia					
Waste management (4, 8, 17, 20)	ENR HUD INT EOP EPA OTA	CRE EEO LMB STP	CO SC TR	EP	VA
Water pollution (8, 16, 17)	COM EPA	NOAA	CO, RE, SC, TR	CO EP	COM VA
Water power (4, 7)	INT TVA	RB	CO, RE, TR	EN EP	ENER
Water rights (14, 16)	INT JUS	RB LNR	RE	EN	ENER
Water supply (11, 16, 17)	AGR INT INT TVA	SCS GS RB	AG CO RE TR	AG EN EP	ENER INT
Water transportation (2, 17, 19)	TRA TRA FMC ICC	CG MA	CO SC TR	CO EP	COM
Waterways. See Inland waterways					
Weapons (15, 17)	DEF DEF ENR EOP OTA	DNA REO DPO STP	NS	AR	DEF ENER
Weather (1, 8, 17)	COM NSF	NWS	SC	CO	COM VA
Weights and measures (2, 17)	COM	NIST	SC	CO	COM
Welfare (9, 12, 18)	HHS LAB SSA	FAO ETA	EE WM	FI LA	LAB
Wheat. See Grains					
Whistleblowers. See Government employees					
White collar crime (14)	DEF JUS JUS TRE TRE PS SEC	DIS FBI JSB IRS SS	BA GR JU	BA GA JU	COM TRE
White House facilities (10)	INT GSA	NPS PBS	RE TR	EP	INT TRE
Wholesale trade. See Economic data					

	PARENTS	SUBUNITS	HOUSE	SENATE	FUNDING
Widowers/widows. See Survivor benefits					
Wilderness areas (5, 16)	AGR INT INT	FS LMB NPS	RE	EN	INT
Wildlife conservation (8, 16)	AGR COM INT INT INT MMC TVA	FS NOAA FWS NPS RB	AG RE	AG EN EP	COM INT
Wiretapping (14)	JUS JUS	EUSA PDO	JU	JU	COM
Witness protection (14)	JUS JUS	EUSA MS	JU	JU	COM

Women. See Abortion, Child
  support, Day care, Discrimination, Family planning,
  Prenatal care

Wood. See Timber resources

Work-study programs.
  See Higher education

Workers compensation (6, 12)	LAB	WCP	EE	LA	LAB

Working conditions. See
  Indoor health, Labor
  standards, Occupational
  safety

World fairs. See Expositions

World health. See Epidemiology,
  Foreign aid, International
  organizations

World migration. See
  Immigration

World peace. See International
  arbitration, International law,
  International organizations

World politics. See Diplomatic
  recognition, National security,
  Treaties

World population. See
  Population growth

Writs. See Court orders

Youth. See Child abuse,
  Juvenile delinquency,
  Missing children

SUBJECT ENTRIES WITH MULTIPLE CROSS REFERENCES

Administrative law: Contempt power, Legislative delegation, Regulatory procedure

Aged: Elderly, Gerontology, Senior citizens

Agricultural research: National libraries, Scientific research, Seeds

Air pollution: Pollution, Smog

Aliens: Foreign residents, Illegal aliens

Antitrust law: Business competition, Corporate mergers, Monopolies

Armed forces: Air Force, Army, Combat readiness, Navy, Overseas posts

Arts: Cultural expression, Performing arts, Visual arts

Atmosphere: Climate, Earth sciences, Ozone layer

Aviation safety: Accidents, Aircraft, Helicopters

Bank deposits: Certificates of deposit, Deposit insurance, Personal finance

Bankruptcy: Business failures, Corporate finance, Defaults

Border patrol: Detention, National borders

Broadcasting: Cable television, Entertainment industry, Equal time, Mass media, Political expression, Radio industry, Television industry

Business investment: Capital formation, Corporate finance

Census: Demographic data, Housing data, Migration, Population data, Poverty level, Socioeconomic data, Statistical data

Civil procedure: Class action, Court costs, Pretrial procedure, Private litigation, Torts

Coastal zone management: Estuaries, Shoreline erosion, Tidelands

Commercial law: Black market, Corporate structure

Communicable diseases: Disease control, Infectious diseases, Influenza, Viruses

Computer technology: Artificial intelligence, Electronic data processing, Engineering, Information science, Software industry

Congressional-executive relations: Political liaison, Presidential-congressional relations, Veto power

Congressional organization: Bicameralism, House of Representatives, Legislative leaders, Political parties, Senate

Congressional power: Confirmations, Contempt power, Interstate commerce, Legislative investigations, State power

Consumer credit: Borrowing, Credit cards

Consumer Price Index: Prices, Purchasing power

Consumer protection: Business ethics, Credit bureaus, Deceptive practices, Fraud, Mail order sales, Telemarketing, Warranties

Copyrights: Authors, Entertainment industry, Intellectual
   property, Magazines, Property rights, Publcations, Royalties,
   Software industry

Court orders: Consent decrees, Habeus corpus, Writs

Credit programs: Government loans, Lending, Subsidies

Crime data: Felonies, Statistical data

Crime victims: Restitution, Victim assistance

Criminal procedure: Detention, Grand juries, Indictments,
   Plea bargaining, Pretrial procedure

Currency: Bank notes, Coinage, Legal tender, Money

Day care: Child care, Women

Debt collection: Defaults, Financial management

Diplomatic service: Consulates, Embassies, Foreign service,
   Overseas posts

Disability benefits: Blindness, Deafness

Disaster relief: Displaced persons, Earthquake damage, Fire
   damage, Flood damage, Hurricanes, Natural disasters, Storms,
   Tornadoes, Victim assistance

Drug abuse: Addiction, Cocaine, Heroin, Marihuana, Narcotics,
   Opiates

Drug safety: Antibiotics, Opiates, Pharmaceutical industry,
   Prescription drugs, Sedatives

Drug testing: Cocaine, Heroin, Marihuana, Narcotics

Drug traffic: Cocaine, Heroin, Marihuana, Narcotics

Eating disorders: Digestive diseases, Obesity

Economic controls: Price controls, Rent control, Wage controls

Economic data: Balance of payments, Business cycles, Consumer
   spending, Employment data, Inflation, Manufacturing, Productivity, Recession, Retail trade, Standard of living, Statistical data, Wholesale trade

Education data: Statistical data, Students

Elections: Campaign finance, Congressional agenda, Political
   fundraising, Political parties, Representation

Eminent domain: Bill of Rights, Private property

Energy research: Geothermal energy, Scientific research,
   Solar energy, Synthetic fuels

Environmental research: Climate, Scientific research

Exports: Embargoes, Foreign markets, Overseas business

Extradition: Detention, Fugitives

Family planning: Birth control, Women

Family services: Adoption, Child custody, Domestic violence,
   Foster care, Orphans

Federal courts: Appellate courts, Constitutional litigation,
   Contempt power, Court rules, District courts, Interjudicial
   relations, Judicial circuits, Judicial power, Statutory
   interpretation, Supreme Court

Federal judges: Chief Justice, Magistrates, Public officials

Federal paperwork: Administrative management, Data collection,
   Records management, Red tape

Federal records: American history, Archives, Genealogy,
   Historical documents

Financial institutions: Electronic fund transfers, Lending,
   Savings and loan associations, Thrift industry

Food inspection: Additives, Contamination

Food stamps: Entitlement programs, Poverty programs

Foreign aid: Developing countries, Displaced persons,
   Humanitarian aid, Overseas posts, World health

Freight: Cargo, Shipping

Fringe benefits: Compensation, Employee benefits

Genetics: Hereditary diseases, Life sciences

Government borrowing: Deficit financing, Fiscal policy,
   Public finance

Government contracts: Contracts, Restitution

Government employees: Civil Service, Partisan activities,
   Public officials, Whistleblowers

Government fellowships: Graduate education, Scholarships

Government information: Censorship, Classified information,
   Freedom of information, Information management

Government liability: Legal immunity, Sovereign immunity

Government procurement: Aerospace industry, Defense industry

Government securities: Bonds, Monetary policy, Mortgage
   securities, Savings bonds, Treasury securities

Government spending: Appropriations, Expenditures, Fiscal
   policy, Public finance

Handicapped: Blindness, Brain disorders, Deafness, Disabled,
   Mental illness, Physical disability, Special education

Health data: Birth rates, Mortality rates, Statistical data

Health insurance: Catastrophic illness, Entitlement programs,
   Medicaid, Medical insurance, Medical malpractice, Medicare,
   Prescription drugs

Higher education: Colleges, Graduate education, Universities,
   Work-study programs

Highway safety: Accidents, Drunk driving, Motor vehicles,
   Traffic accidents

Historic preservation: American history, Archeological sites,
   National landmarks

Horticulture: Flowers, Gardening, Seeds

Housing management: Condominiums, Cooperative housing,
   Rental housing, Subsidized housing, Tenants

Humanities: Cultural expression, Languages, Literature

Imports: Foreign products, Quotas

Indians: Native Americans, Tribal rights

Indoor health: Asbestos, Working conditions

Industrial pollution: Factories, Pollution

Industrial technology: Automation, Engineering, Robotics

Inland waterways: Canals, Lakes, Rivers, Waterways

Inspectors General: Abuse of authority, Administrative management,
   Contracts, Financial management, Fraud, Neglect of duty

Insurance industry: Life insurance, Perosnal finance, Property
   insurance, Storms

Intelligence activities: Counterintelligence, Covert action,
   Spying

Interest rates: Discount rate, Lending, Monetary policy,
   Mortgage securities

Intergovernmental relations: Federalism, Policy implementation,
   State power

International agreements: Cultural exchange, Executive agreements

International finance: Devaluation, Foreign debts

International law: Admiralty law, Laws of war, World peace

International organizations: Peacekeeping forces, United
   Nations, World health, World peace

International travel: Passports, Visas

Judicial administration: Court employees, Court records

Judicial remedies: Declaratory judgments, Equitable relief,
   Injunctions, Restitution

Labor relations: Arbitration, Industrial relations, Lockouts,
   Strikes

Labor standards: Factories, Working conditions

Law enforcement: Criminal investigations, Police forces,
   Searches and seizures

Legal services: Bill of Rights, Public defenders

Libraries: Information resources, National libraries, Publications

Lobbying: Congressional agenda, Interest groups, Political
   expression

Local governments: Cities, Counties, Metropolitan areas,
   Municipalities

Mapping: Cartography, Geography, Topography

Marine safety: Accidents, Boating

Maritime industry: Admiralty law, Fishing, Merchant marine, Shipping

Mass transit: Public transportation, Subways

Medical research: Human subjects, Life sciences, National libraries, Opiates, Scientific research

Members of Congress: Conflicts of interest, Congressional ethics, Constituent services, Political parties, Public officials, Representatives, Senators

Mental health: Depression, Phobias, Psychological disorders, Sleep disorders, Suicide

Military assistance: Overseas conflicts, Peacekeeping forces

Military law: Courts-martial, Police forces

Military research: Nuclear deterrence, Scientific research

Missing children: Child abduction, Runaways, Youth

Money supply: Bank reserves, Checking accounts, Monetary policy, Open market operations

Mortgage loans: Home mortgages, Housing rehabilitation

National security: Intervention abroad, Military strategy, Nuclear deterrence, Peacekeeping forces, World politics

Natural gas: Fuel, Gas

Negotiable instruments: Checks, Commercial paper, Money orders

Neurological diseases: Brain disorders, Headaches, Memory loss, Paralysis, Stroke

Neutrality law: Laws of war, Overseas conflicts

Nonprofit organizations: Cultural expression, Foundations

Nuclear energy: Atomic energy, Uranium

Numismatics: Coins, Commemorative medals

Nutrition: Calories, Diet, Health food, Salt, Vitamins

Occupational safety: Accidents, Factories, Industrial safety, Working conditions

Patents: Inventions, Property rights, Royalties

Pensions: Annuities, Compensation, Entitlement programs, Personal finance

Petroleum: Fuel, Gasoline, Oil

Population growth: Birth control, World population

Precious metals: Gold, Silver

Precious stones: Diamonds, Gems

Prenatal care: Birth defects, Childbirth, Women

Presidency: Commander in Chief, Congressional agenda, Executive power, National emergencies, Nominations, Vice-Presidency

Privacy: Bill of Rights, Confidential data, Data banks,
   Electronic surveillance, Freedom of information, Personal
   data, Vital records

Product labeling: Apparel industry, Prescription drugs

Product safety: Accidents, Bicycles, Defective products,
   Flammable materials, Recalls, Toys

Proprietary data: Freedom of information, Trade secrets

Public administration: Administrative management, Contracts,
   Information management

Public debt: Bonds, National debt, Public finance

Recording industry: Audio equipment, Entertainment industry,
   Home entertainment, Tape recordings, Video equipment

Recreation areas: Beaches, Campgrounds, Outdoor recreation,
   Parks, Seashores

Securities industry: Bonds, Borrowing, Brokerage firms,
   Corporate finance, Financial markets, Investment companies,
   Mortgage securities, Municipal and state bonds, Mutual funds,
   Personal finance, Stock markets

Sentences: Bill of rights, Judicial punishment, Probation

Separation of powers: Constitutional structure, Interbranch
   relations

Sports: Athletics, Olympic games

Student loans: Education assistance, Graduate education,
   Tuition

Taxation: Business income, Corporate finance, Dividends,
   Earned income credit, Estates and trusts, Excises, Fiscal
   policy, Income tax, Interest payments, Investment income,
   Partnerships, Payroll taxes, Public finance, Revenue, Tax
   evasion, Tax expenditures

Telecommunications: Citizens band radio, Internet, Telephone
   service

Territorial waters: National borders, Shoreline patrol

Tourism: Travel industry, Vacations

Toxic substances: Contamination, Poisons

Trade agreements: Free trade, Most Favored Nation Status,
   Trade disputes and remedies

Trademarks: Brand names, Property rights

Trials: Bill of Rights, Pretrial procedure

Visual disorders: Blindness, Eye care

Wages: Compensation, Minimum wage

Waste management: Incinerators, Landfills, Pollution,
   Recycling, Sanitation, Sewage treatment, Solid waste,
   Trash

Water pollution: Contamination, Pollution

Water supply: Drinking water, Rainfall, Reservoirs, Saline water

Water transportation: Ferries, Shipping

Weapons: Armament, Missiles, Munitions, Nuclear deterrence

Weather: Climate, Meteorology, Rainfall, Storms

Welfare: Aid to Families with Dependent Children (AFDC), Entitlement programs, Job training, Poverty programs

White collar crime: Computer crime, Fraud

Wildlife conservation: Conservation, Fish, Hunting

Workers compensation: Employer liability, Victim assistance

Part 2

General Subject Categories

SPECIFIC SUBJECT CATEGORIES BY GENERAL SUBJECT CATEGORY

AGRICULTURE (1)

Agricultural credit

Agricultural development

Agricultural markets

Agricultural production

Agricultural research

Agricultural subsidies

Agricultural surpluses

Commodity markets

Crops

Dairy industry

Economic data

Fibers

Fruits

Grains

Herbicides

Horticulture

Insects

Irrigation

Land management

Livestock

Meat

Pesticides

Plants

Poultry

Rural areas

Soil conservation

Sugar

Tobacco industry

Weather

COMMERCE (2)

Advertising

Alcoholic beverages

Antitrust law

Automobile industry

Aviation industry

Billboards

Broadcasting

Bus lines

Business assistance

Business regulation

Commercial credit

Commercial law

Commodity markets

Consumer protection

Correspondence courses

Economic controls

Economic data

Energy consumption

Energy prices

Energy production

Environmental liability

Exports

Expositions

Foreign investments

Franchises

Freight

Gross Domestic Product

Ground transportation

Harbors

Imports

Industrial technology

Inland waterways

Insurance industry

Interest rates

International communication

International trade

COMMERCE (2)

International transportation

Land sales

Lotteries

Maritime industry

Medical laboratories

Mineral leases

Mining industry

Moving industry

Multinational corporations

Negotiable instruments

Numismatics

Panama Canal

Passenger ships

Philately

Pipelines

Plastics

Postal Service

Precious metals

Precious stones

Product labeling

Product liability

Proprietary data

Railroad industry

Recording industry

Resource shortages

Rural areas

Securities industry

Small business

Space commercialization

Sports

Tariffs

Technology transfer

Telecommunications

Tourism

Trade agreements

Trade deficits

Trademarks

Trucking industry

Water transportation

COMMUNICATION (3)

Advertising

Arts

Billboards

Broadcasting

Charitable organizations

Computer technology

Copyrights

Federal records

Government information

Government publications

International communication

Journalistic confidentiality

Nonprofit organizations

Obscenity

Postal Service

Privacy

Proprietary data

Public broadcasting

Public demonstrations

Recording industry

Religious institutions

Space communication

Telecommunications

COMMUNITY DEVELOPMENT (4)

Agricultural development

Airports

Bridges

COMMUNITY DEVELOPMENT (4)

Business assistance

Credit programs

Dams

Depressed areas

Disaster relief

Harbors

Highway construction

Inland waterways

Insurance programs

Land sales

Military installations

Public buildings

Public housing

Real estate industry

Rural areas

Small business

Tunnels

Waste management

Water power

EDUCATION (5)

Adult education

Architecture

Arts

Bilingual education

Compensatory education

Consumer education

Correspondence courses

Crime prevention

Education data

Education research

Elementary education

Ethnic groups

Government fellowships

Higher education

Historic preservation

Home economics

Humanities

Juvenile delinquency

Learning disabilities

Libraries

Literacy

Monuments

Museums

Nonprofit organizations

Numismatics

Nutrition

Philately

Physical education

Preschool education

Preventive medicine

Private schools

Public broadcasting

Public schools

Rehabilitation services

Secondary education

Service academies

Social sciences

Sports

Student loans

Veterans

Vocational education

Volunteer services

Wilderness areas

EMPLOYMENT (6)

Aliens

Apprenticeship

Child labor

EMPLOYMENT (6)

Congressional employees

Day care

Drug testing

Economic data

Fringe benefits

Government employees

Indoor health

Labor markets

Labor relations

Labor standards

Marine safety

Migrant workers

Mine safety

Occupational safety

Pensions

Polygraphs

Radiation

Retirement

Unemployment compensation

Unemployment rate

Veterans

Vocational education

Vocational rehabilitation

Wages

Workers compensation

ENERGY (7)

Coal

Electric power

Energy conservation

Energy consumption

Energy data

Energy prices

Energy production

Energy research

Energy storage

Hydroelectric power

Mineral leases

Natural gas

Nuclear energy

Nuclear facilities

Offshore drilling

Outer continental shelf

Petroleum

Pipelines

Public utilities

Resource shortages

Underground exploration

Water power

ENVIRONMENTAL AFFAIRS (8)

Acid rain

Air pollution

Atmosphere

Coal

Earthquake research

Energy storage

Environmental protection

Environmental research

Flood control

Global environment

Hazardous materials

Herbicides

Hydroelectric power

Industrial pollution

Marine resources

Mineral resources

Mining industry

Noise pollution

ENVIRONMENTAL AFFAIRS (8)

Nuclear facilities

Nuclear safety

Nuclear waste

Ocean policy

Oceanography

Oil spills

Pesticides

Petroleum

Pipelines

Population growth

Public lands

Public utilities

Radiation

Radon

Recreation areas

Rights-of-way

Technology transfer

Territorial waters

Timber resources

Toxic substances

Waste management

Water pollution

Weather

Wildlife conservation

FINANCIAL AFFAIRS (9)

Accounting

Agricultural credit

Bank deposits

Bank regulation

Bankruptcy

Budget administration

Budget deficits

Budget formulation

Business assistance

Commercial credit

Consumer credit

Consumer Price Index

Credit programs

Credit unions

Currency

Customs

Debt collection

Debt management

Economic controls

Economic data

Financial institutions

Foreclosure

Foreign currency

Foreign investments

Foreign taxes

Funding gaps

Government borrowing

Government securities

Government spending

Gross Domestic Product

Health insurance

Housing industry

Impoundments

Individual retirement
  accounts

Interest rates

International finance

Local governments

Money laundering

Money supply

Mortgage loans

Multinational corporations

Negotiable instruments

Pensions

Precious metals

FINANCIAL AFFAIRS (9)

Public debt

Real estate industry

Revenue sharing

Securities industry

Social Security

State governments

Student loans

Tariffs

Taxation

Trust funds

Welfare

GOVERNMENTAL AFFAIRS (10)

Accounting

Administrative law

Advisory committees

Architecture

Budget administration

Budget deficits

Budget formulation

Capitol facilities

Census

Citizenship

Civil-military relations

Congressional districts

Congressional employees

Congressional operations

Congressional organization

Congressional oversight

Congressional power

Congressional-executive relations

Corrupt practices

Currency

Debt management

Diplomatic service

District of Columbia

Elections

Eminent domain

Ethnic groups

Executive branch
    operations

Executive branch
    organization

Executive orders

Executive privilege

Federal courts

Federal judges

Federal paperwork

Federal property

Federal records

Flag of the U.S.

Funding gaps

Government borrowing

Government contracts

Government corporations

Government employees

Government ethics

Government information

Government procurement

Government publications

Government securities

Government spending

Holidays

Identity papers

Impeachment

Impoundments

Inspectors General

Interagency relations

Intergovernmental relations

Interstate relations

GOVERNMENTAL AFFAIRS (10)

Judicial administration

Legal opinions

Lobbying

Local governments

Lotteries

Mapping

Medal of Freedom

Members of Congress

Money supply

Naturalization

Pensions

Physical security

Political asylum

Postal Service

Presidency

Public administration

Public buildings

Public debt

Revenue sharing

Seal of the U.S.

Separation of powers

Space exploration

State boundaries

State governments

Taxation

Territories

Voting

War powers

White House facilities

HEALTH (11)

Abortion

Acquired immune deficiency
  syndrome (AIDS)

Air pollution

Alcoholism

Allergies

Animals

Arthritis

Automobile industry

Aviation safety

Bacteriology

Blood

Building standards

Burn injuries

Cancer

Chemicals

Child health

Communicable diseases

Construction industry

Consumer protection

Cosmetics industry

Dentistry

Drug abuse

Drug safety

Drug testing

Eating disorders

Environmental liability

Environmental protection

Epidemiology

Explosives

Food inspection

Fruits

Handicapped

Hazardous materials

Health care

Health data

Health insurance

Health maintenance
  organizations

Hearing disorders

HEALTH (11)

Heart disease

Herbicides

Highway safety

Hospital facilities

Hospital regulation

Immunization

Indoor health

Industrial pollution

Infant mortality

Marine safety

Meat

Medical devices

Medical laboratories

Medical research

Mental health

Mine safety

Mobile homes

Neurological diseases

Nuclear safety

Nursing homes

Nutrition

Occupational safety

Organ transplants

Orthopedics

Pesticides

Physical education

Population growth

Prenatal care

Preventive medicine

Product labeling

Product safety

Product tampering

Radiation

Radon

Railroad safety

Rehabilitation services

Respiratory diseases

Skin diseases

Smoking

Sugar

Toxic substances

Trauma

Venereal disease

Veterans

Visual disorders

Water supply

INCOME SECURITY (12)

Aged

Agricultural credit

Agricultural subsidies

Child support

Crime victims

Crops

Disability benefits

Disaster relief

Food stamps

Fringe benefits

Handicapped

Homelessness

Housing management

Insurance programs

Pensions

Retirement

Social Security

Survivor benefits

Trust funds

Unemployment compensation

Veterans

INCOME SECURITY (12)

Welfare

Workers compensation

INTERNATIONAL AFFAIRS (13)

Agricultural development

Agricultural markets

Agricultural surpluses

Airspace

Arms control

Arms exports

Border patrol

Citizens abroad

Customs

Diplomatic immunity

Diplomatic recognition

Diplomatic service

Disaster relief

Drug traffic

Espionage

Exports

Expositions

Extradition

Food distribution

Foreign agents

Foreign aid

Foreign currency

Foreign investments

Foreign property

Foreign sovereign immunity

Foreign taxes

Foreign visitors

Global environment

Human rights

Hunger

Immigration

Imports

Intelligence activities

International agreeemnts

International arbitration

International boundaries

International claims

International communication

International crime

International finance

International law

International organizations

International trade

International transportation

International travel

International waters

Maritime industry

Martial law

Military assistance

Multinational corporations

National security

Neutrality law

North Atlantic Treaty
Organization (NATO)

Nuclear proliferation

Ocean policy

Panama Canal

Polar regions

Political asylum

Population growth

Refugees

Repatriation

Resource shortages

Salvage

Tariffs

Technology transfer

INTERNATIONAL AFFAIRS (13)

Terrorism

Trade agreements

Trade deficits

Treason

Treaties

War powers

Warfare

LEGAL AFFAIRS (14)

Abortion

Administrative law

Alcoholic beverages

Aliens

Antitrust law

Arson

Bankruptcy

Border patrol

Capital punishment

Citizenship

Civil disorders

Civil procedure

Civil rights

Commercial law

Computer security

Congressional power

Congressional-executive relations

Constitutional amendments

Consumer credit

Copyrights

Correctional facilities

Corrupt practices

Counterfeiting

Court orders

Crime data

Crime victims

Criminal procedure

Deportation

Diplomatic immunity

Discrimination

Drug traffic

Eminent domain

Environmental liability

Espionage

Executive orders

Executive privilege

Expatriation

Explosives

Extradition

Federal charters

Federal courts

Federal judges

Firearms

Foreclosure

Foreign agents

Foreign sovereign immunity

Gambling

Government ethics

Government liability

Government litigation

Hate crimes

Hijacking

Identity papers

Immigration

Impeachment

Industrial security

International claims

International crime

International law

Interstate relations

LEGAL AFFAIRS (14)

Journalistic confidentiality

Judicial administration

Judicial ethics

Judicial remedies

Juries

Juvenile delinquency

Law enforcement

Legal opinions

Legal services

Lobbying

Money laundering

Naturalization

Neutrality law

Obscenity

Obstruction of justice

Organized crime

Pardons

Parole

Patents

Police misconduct

Polygraphs

Pornography

Prisoners

Privacy

Product liability

Product tampering

Public demonstrations

Recording Industry

Refugees

Salvage

Seal of the U.S.

Sentences

Separation of powers

Smuggling

Subversive activities

Terrorism

Tobacco industry

Trademarks

Treason

Treaties

Trials

Violent crime

Voting

War powers

Water rights

White collar crime

Wiretapping

Witness protection

NATIONAL DEFENSE (15)

Airspace

Armed forces

Arms control

Arms exports

Civil defense

Government contracts

Industrial security

Intelligence activities

International agreements

International waters

Marine Corps

Martial law

Medal of Honor

Military assistance

Military installations

Military law

Military operations

Military personnel

Military research

NATIONAL DEFENSE (15)

National Guard

National security

North Atlantic Treaty
    Organization (NATO)

Nuclear proliferation

Nuclear testing

Panama Canal

Selective Service

Service academies

Space communication

Strategic stockpiles

Subversive activities

Territorial waters

Terrorism

Treaties

Warfare

Weapons

NATURAL RESOURCES (16)

Acid rain

Air pollution

Animals

Birds

Coal

Coastal zone management

Dams

Endangered species

Fire control

Flood control

Forestry

Geology

Grazing lands

Historic preservation

Indians

Inland waterways

Insects

Irrigation

Land management

Mapping

Marine resources

Maritime industry

Mineral leases

Mineral resources

Natural gas

Nuclear energy

Ocean policy

Oceanography

Outer continental shelf

Petroleum

Plants

Precious metals

Precious stones

Public lands

Recreation areas

Resource shortages

Soil conservation

Strategic stockpiles

Timber resources

Underground exploration

Undersea exploration

Water pollution

Water rights

Water supply

Wilderness areas

Wildlife conservation

SCIENCE & TECHNOLOGY (17)

Aeronautics

Agricultural research

Air pollution

SCIENCE & TECHNOLOGY

Astronomy

Atmosphere

Aviation safety

Biotechnology

Building standards

Chemicals

Coastal zone management

Computer security

Computer technology

Drug safety

Drug testing

Earthquake research

Electric power

Electrical standards

Energy conservation

Energy production

Energy research

Environmental research

Explosives

Fire control

Genetics

Geology

Global environment

Ground transportation

Highway safety

Industrial technology

Laboratory research

Marine resources

Medical devices

Medical research

Military research

Noise pollution

Nuclear energy

Nuclear testing

Nuclear waste

Oceanography

Offshore drilling

Organ transplants

Patents

Pipelines

Plastics

Polar regions

Privacy

Product safety

Radiation

Railroad safety

Recording industry

Soil conservation

Space commercialization

Space communication

Space exploration

Technological risk

Technology transfer

Telecommunications

Underground exploration

Undersea exploration

Waste management

Water pollution

Water supply

Water transportation

Weapons

Weather

Weights and measures

SOCIAL SERVICES (18)

Aged

Agricultural surpluses

Charitable organizations

Child abuse

SOCIAL SERVICES (18)

Child health

Child nutrition

Child support

Day care

Disability benefits

Family planning

Family services

Food distribution

Handicapped

Homelessness

Hospital regulation

Hunger

Indians

Learning disabilities

Migrant workers

Missing children

Nursing homes

Prenatal care

Refugees

Rehabilitation services

Religious institutions

Retirement

Social Security

Survivor benefits

Vocational rehabilitation

Volunteer services

Welfare

TRANSPORTATION (19)

Aeronautics

Airports

Automobile industry

Aviation industry

Bridges

Bus lines

Freight

Ground transportation

Harbors

Highway construction

Highway safety

Hijacking

Inland waterways

International transportation

Marine safety

Mass transit

Mobile homes

Moving industry

Ocean policy

Oil spills

Passenger ships

Railroad industry

Railroad safety

Rescue services

Rights-of-way

Time zones

Trucking industry

Tunnels

Water transportation

URBAN AFFAIRS (20)

Building standards

Construction industry

Credit programs

Depressed areas

District of Columbia

Homelessness

Homesteading

Housing industry

Housing management

URBAN AFFAIRS (20)

Insurance programs

Intergovernmental relations

Land sales

Local governments

Mass transit

Mortgage loans

Public housing

Real estate industry

Slum clearance

Small business

Waste management

PARENT AGENCIES AND COMMITTEES BY GENERAL SUBJECT CATEGORY

	PARENTS	HOUSE		SENATE	FUNDING
AGRICULTURE (1)	AGR CFTC FCA	AG	(JEC)	AG	AGR
COMMERCE (2)	CFTC COM CPSC ENR EXIM FCC FMC FRB FTC ICC IDCA ITC JUS PCC SBA SEC STA TRA TRE	AG BA CO IR JU RE SB SC WM	(JEC)	AG BA CO EN EP FI FR JU SB	AGR COM ENER FO TRA TRE VA
COMMUNICATION (3)	COM EDU EOP FCC FTC JUS NARA NFAH PRC PS STA USIA	CO EE GR IR JU SC		CO FR GA JU LA	COM INT LAB TRE
COMMUNITY DEVELOPMENT (4)	AGR COM DEF FEMA SBA TRA TVA	AG CO NS SB TR		AG AR CO EP SB	AGR COM MC TRA VA
EDUCATION (5)	ACTION CPSC EDU FAC GPO LC NCLIS NCSC NFAH NSF SI USIP VA	EE HO RE VA		EN LA RU VA	INT LAB LEG VA

	PARENTS	HOUSE	SENATE	FUNDING
EMPLOYMENT (6)	EEOC	EE	AGI	LAB
	FLRA	GR	GA	TRE
	FMCS	VA	LA	
	FMSH		VA	
	LAB	(JEC)		
	NLRB			
	NMB			
	OPM			
	OSHR			
	PBGC			
	VA			
ENERGY (7)	DEF	CO	AR	DEF
	ENR	NS	EN	ENER
	INT	RE	EP	INT
	NRC	SC		
	TVA	TR	(JEC)	
ENVIRONMENTAL	COM	CO	CO	COM
AFFAIRS (8)	ENR	RE	EN	ENER
	EOP	SC	EP	INT
	EPA	TR		TRA
	FEMA			VA
	INT			
	MMC			
	TRA			
FINANCIAL AFFAIRS (9)	AGR	AG	AG	AGR
	CBO	BA	BA	COM
	COM	BU	BU	FO
	EOP	CO	CO	LEG
	FCA	GR	FI	TRE
	FDIC	IR	FR	VA
	FRB	VA	GA	
	FTC	WM	VA	
	GAO	(JEC)		
	HUD			
	IDCA			
	NCUA			
	PBGC			
	SEC			
	SSA			
	TRE			
	VA			
GOVERNMENTAL	ACIR	DA	BA	COM
AFFAIRS (10)	ACUS	BU	BU	INT
	ARC	GR	DI	LEG
	CBO	HO	ET	TRE
	COM	IR	FI	
	EOP	JU	FR	
	FAC	RE	GA	
	FEC	RU	JU	
	FLRA	ST	RU	
	FRB	WM		
	GAO	(JCP)		
	GEO			
	GPO			
	GSA			
	JUS			
	LC			
	MSPB			

	PARENTS	HOUSE	SENATE	FUNDING
GOVERNMENTAL AFFAIRS (10)	NARA NCPC OPM PADC PRC PS SCO STA TRE			
HEALTH (11)	AGR CPSC EPA FMSH HHS LAB NRC NTSB OSHR TRA VA	AG CO EE RE VA WM	AG AGI CO EP FI LA VA	AGR ENER LAB TRA VA
INCOME SECURITY (12)	AGR FEMA HHS HUD LAB OPM PBGC SSA TRE VA	AG BA BU EE GR VA WM (JEC)	AG AGI BA BU FI GA LA VA	AGR LAB TRE VA
INTERNATIONAL AFFAIRS (13)	ACDA AGR COM DEF EOP EXIM FCC FMC FRB IDCA ITC PCC PCO SCEC STA TRA TRE USIA USIP	AG BA CO IN IR NS WM	AG AR BA CO FI FR INT	AGR COM DEF FO TRA TRE
LEGAL AFFAIRS (14)	ACUS CRC EEOC FCC FEC FTC JUS LSC STA TRE	CO GR HO IR JU	CO FR GA JU RU	COM LEG TRE

	PARENTS	HOUSE	SENATE	FUNDING
NATIONAL DEFENSE (15)	ACDA	CO	AR	COM
	DEF	IN	EN	DEF
	ENR	IR	FR	ENER
	EOP	NS	INT	MC
	FEMA			
	PCC			
	SSS			
	STA			
NATURAL RESOURCES (16)	AGR	AG	AG	AGR
	COM	CO	AR	COM
	DEF	NS	EN	ENER
	ENR	RE	EP	INT
	EPA	TR	IN	VA
	INT			
	MMC			
	TVA			
SCIENCE & TECHNOLOGY (17)	AGR	AG	AG	AGR
	COM	CO	AR	COM
	DEF	EE	CO	DEF
	ENR	NS	EN	ENER
	EOP	RE	EP	INT
	HHS	SC	LA	LAB
	INT	TR		VA
	NASA			
	NSF			
	OTA			
	SI			
	TRA			
SOCIAL SERVICES (18)	ACTION	AG	AG	AGR
	AGR	BA	AGI	LAB
	EDU	CO	BA	VA
	HHS	EE	FI	
	HUD	VA	IN	
	LAB	WM	LA	
	NCSC		VA	
	SSA			
	VA			
TRANSPORTATION (19)	FMC	CO	CO	COM
	ICC	IR	EP	TRA
	NASA	SC	FR	VA
	NTSB	TR		
	STA			
	TRA			
URBAN AFFAIRS (20)	HUD	BA	BA	DC
	NCPC	GR	EP	INT
	PADC	RE	GA	VA
	SBA	SB	GB	
	TRA	TR		

Part 3

Parent Agencies

SPECIFIC SUBJECT CATEGORIES BY PARENT AGENCY

ACTION

Literacy

Volunteer services

Administrative Conference
of the United States

Administrative law

Public administration

Advisory Commission on
Intergovernmental Relations

Intergovernmental relations

Local governments

State governments

Agriculture Department

Agricultural credit

Agricultural development

Agricultural markets

Agricultural production

Agricultural research

Agricultural subsidies

Agricultural surpluses

Animals

Birds

Child nutrition

Consumer education

Crops

Dairy industry

Disaster relief

Economic data

Endangered species

Environmental protection

Exports

Fibers

Fire control

Flood control

Food distribution

Food inspection

Food stamps

Foreclosure

Foreign aid

Forestry

Fruits

Grains

Herbicides

Home economics

Horticulture

Hunger

Insects

International trade

Irrigation

Land management

Livestock

Meat

Nutrition

Pesticides

Plants

Poultry

Product tampering

Public lands

Recreation areas

Rural areas

Soil conservation

Sugar

Timber resources

Tobacco industry

Agriculture Department

Water supply

Wilderness areas

Wildlife conservation

Architect of the Capitol

Capitol facilities

Arms Control and
Disarmament Agency

Arms control

Arms exports

Nuclear proliferation

Nuclear testing

Civil Rights Commission

Civil rights

Voting

Commerce Department

Air pollution

Atmosphere

Biotechnology

Broadcasting

Building standards

Business assistance

Business investment

Census

Chemicals

Coastal zone management

Computer security

Computer technology

Congressional districts

Customs

Depressed areas

Economic data

Electrical standards

Endangered species

Energy conservation

Environmental protection

Environmental research

Ethnic groups

Exports

Expositions

Fire control

Flood control

Food inspection

Foreign investments

Franchises

Government publications

Gross Domestic Product

Harbors

Imports

Industrial technology

International finance

International trade

International travel

Laboratory research

Local governments

Mapping

Marine resources

Mineral leases

Multinational corporations

Neutrality law

Ocean policy

Oceanography

Offshore drilling

Patents

Plastics

Population growth

Precious stones

Commerce Department

Product safety

Public broadcasting

Radiation

Resource shortages

Revenue sharing

Small business

Space commercialization

State governments

Strategic stockpiles

Tariffs

Technology transfer

Telecommunications

Territorial waters

Tourism

Trade agreements

Trade deficits

Trademarks

Undersea exploration

Water pollution

Weather

Weights and measures

Wildlife conservation

Commodity Futures
Trading Commission

Commodity markets

Precious metals

Sugar

Congressional Budget Office

Budget deficits

Budget formulation

Credit programs

Economic data

Government spending

Health insurance

Pensions

Public debt

Social Security

Taxation

Trust funds

Consumer Product
Safety Commission

Consumer education

Consumer protection

Explosives

Hazardous materials

Plastics

Product labeling

Product liability

Product safety

Toxic substances

Defense Department

Airspace

Armed forces

Arms control

Arms exports

Astronomy

Civil defense

Coastal zone management

Dams

Drug testing

Drug traffic

Exports

Flood control

Government contracts

Government procurement

Industrial security

Inland waterways

Defense Department

Intelligence activities

International waters

Mapping

Marine Corps

Martial law

Medal of Honor

Military assistance

Military installations

Military law

Military operations

Military personnel

Military research

National Guard

National security

North Atlantic Treaty
  Organization (NATO)

Nuclear proliferation

Nuclear testing

Ocean policy

Oceanography

Polygraphs

Privacy

Service academies

Space communication

Strategic stockpiles

Technology transfer

Telecommunications

Terrorism

Undersea exploration

Wages

Warfare

Weapons

White collar crime

Education Department

Adult education

Bilingual education

Compensatory education

Correspondence courses

Discrimination

Education data

Education research

Elementary education

Handicapped

Higher education

Home economics

Homelessness

Indians

Juvenile delinquency

Learning disabilities

Libraries

Literacy

Migrant workers

Preschool education

Private schools

Public schools

Rehabilitation services

Secondary education

Sports

Student loans

Veterans

Vocational education

Vocational rehabilitation

Energy Department

Arms control

Coal

Electric power

Energy Department

Energy conservation

Energy consumption

Energy data

Energy prices

Energy production

Energy research

Energy storage

Environmental research

Exports

Hydroelectric power

Industrial security

National security

Natural gas

Nuclear energy

Nuclear facilities

Nuclear proliferation

Nuclear safety

Nuclear testing

Nuclear waste

Offshore drilling

Petroleum

Pipelines

Proprietary data

Public utilities

Radiation

Resource shortages

Strategic stockpiles

Underground exploration

Waste management

Weapons

Environmental Protection Agency

Acid rain

Air pollution

Atmosphere

Automobile industry

Chemicals

Energy storage

Environmental liability

Environmental protection

Environmental research

Hazardous materials

Herbicides

Indoor health

Industrial pollution

Mining industry

Noise pollution

Oil spills

Pesticides

Radiation

Radon

Technology transfer

Toxic substances

Waste management

Water pollution

Equal Employment Opportunity Commission

Apprenticeship

Discrimination

Vocational rehabilitation

Executive Office of the President

Accounting

Acid rain

Aeronautics

Arms control

Biotechnology

Budget administration

Executive Office
of the President

Budget deficits

Budget formulation

Business investment

Civil-military relations

Commercial credit

Computer security

Computer technology

Congressional-executive relations

Consumer credit

Credit programs

Customs

Debt collection

Debt management

Diplomatic recognition

Drug testing

Drug traffic

Economic controls

Economic data

Energy production

Energy research

Environmental research

Espionage

Executive branch operations

Executive branch organization

Executive orders

Executive privilege

Exports

Federal paperwork

Financial institutions

Flag of the U.S.

Foreign aid

Foreign currency

Foreign taxes

Funding gaps

Genetics

Global environment

Government borrowing

Government corporations

Government information

Government procurement

Government spending

Gross Domestic Product

Imports

Impoundments

Industrial pollution

Industrial technology

Inspectors General

Intelligence activities

Interagency relations

Interest rates

Intergovernmental relations

International finance

International trade

Mapping

Marine resources

Martial law

Medal of Freedom

Military assistance

Mineral resources

Multinational corporations

National security

North Atlantic Treaty
  Organization (NATO)

Nuclear energy

Nuclear proliferation

Nuclear waste

Oceanography

Pardons

Presidency

Privacy

**Executive Office
of the President**

Public administration

Public debt

Radiation

Space communication

Space exploration

Tariffs

Taxation

Technological risk

Telecommunications

Terrorism

Trade agreements

Trade deficits

Trust funds

Underground exploration

Undersea exploration

War powers

Warfare

Waste management

Weapons

**Export-Import Bank
of the United States**

Business assistance

Exports

International finance

Farm Credit Administration

Agricultural credit

**Federal Communications
Commission**

Advertising

Antitrust law

Broadcasting

Business regulation

International communication

Obscenity

Public broadcasting

Recording industry

Space communication

Telecommunications

**Federal Deposit Insurance
Corporation**

Bank deposits

Consumer credit

Financial institutions

Money laundering

Negotiable instruments

Federal Election Commission

Elections

Presidency

**Federal Emergency
Management Agency**

Arson

Business assistance

Civil defense

Civil disorders

Crime victims

Disaster relief

Fire control

Homelessness

Insurance programs

Nuclear safety

Radiation

Small business

Strategic stockpiles

Federal Housing Finance Board

Bank regulation

Consumer credit

Financial institutions

Mortgage loans

Federal Labor Relations Authority

Government employees

Labor relations

Federal Maritime Commission

Freight

Harbors

International trade

International transportation

Maritime industry

Passenger ships

Water transportation

Federal Mediation and Conciliation Service

Labor relations

Federal Mine Safety and Health Review Commission

Mine safety

Federal Reserve System

Bank regulation

Consumer credit

Credit unions

Currency

Economic data

Financial institutions

Foreign currency

Government securities

Insurance industry

Interest rates

International finance

Money laundering

Money supply

Negotiable instruments

Precious metals

Securities industry

Federal Trade Commission

Advertising

Antitrust law

Automobile industry

Business regulation

Commercial law

Consumer credit

Consumer education

Consumer protection

Correspondence courses

Debt collection

Franchises

Insurance industry

Land sales

Lotteries

Product labeling

Product safety

Proprietary data

Smoking

Sports

Fine Arts Commission

Architecture

Monuments

Public buildings

General Accounting Office

Accounting

Budget administration

Congressional operations

Congressional oversight

Congressional-executive relations

Credit programs

Debt collection

Debt management

Executive branch operations

Government contracts

Government corporations

Government liability

Government spending

Impoundments

Inspectors General

Interagency relations

Intergovernmental relations

Legal opinions

Public administration

General Services
Administration

Advisory committees

Architecture

Computer security

Computer technology

Consumer education

Executive branch operations

Federal charters

Federal property

Government contracts

Government information

Government procurement

Physical security

Public administration

Public buildings

Small business

Strategic stockpiles

White House facilities

Government Ethics Office

Government ethics

Government Printing Office

Government publications

Libraries

Health and Human
Services Department

Abortion

Acquired immune deficiency
  syndrome (AIDS)

Advertising

Aged

Alcoholism

Allergies

Animals

Arthritis

Bacteriology

Biotechnology

Blood

Burn injuries

Cancer

Child abuse

Child health

Child support

Communicable diseases

Consumer education

Cosmetics industry

Day care

Dentistry

100 Parent Agencies

Health and Human Services Department

Discrimination

Drug abuse

Drug safety

Drug testing

Eating disorders

Environmental research

Epidemiology

Family planning

Family services

Food inspection

Genetics

Handicapped

Health care

Health data

Health insurance

Health maintenance
  organizations

Hearing disorders

Heart disease

Herbicides

Homelessness

Hospital facilities

Hospital regulation

Immunization

Indians

Infant mortality

Juvenile delinquency

Learning disabilities

Medical devices

Medical laboratories

Medical research

Mental health

Migrant workers

Missing children

Neurological diseases

Nursing homes

Nutrition

Occupational safety

Organ transplants

Orthopedics

Pesticides

Physical education

Population growth

Prenatal care

Preschool education

Preventive medicine

Product labeling

Product safety

Product tampering

Radiation

Refugees

Rahabilitation services

Respiratory diseases

Skin diseases

Smoking

Student loans

Sugar

Toxic substances

Trauma

Venereal disease

Visual disorders

Welfare

Housing and Urban Development Department

Building standards

Construction industry

Depressed areas

Discrimination

Housing and Urban
Development Department

Energy conservation

Environmental research

Foreclosure

Homelessness

Homesteading

Housing industry

Housing management

Indians

Insurance programs

Land management

Land sales

Mobile homes

Mortgage loans

Nursing homes

Public housing

Real estate industry

Slum clearance

Waste management

Interior Department

Animals

Architecture

Birds

Coal

Dams

Earthquake research

Endangered species

Energy production

Energy research

Environmental protection

Ethnic groups

Flood control

Forestry

Geology

Grazing lands

Historic preservation

Hydroelectric power

Indians

Inland waterways

Irrigation

Land management

Mapping

Marine resources

Mine safety

Mineral leases

Mineral resources

Mining industry

Monuments

Natural gas

Offshore drilling

Outer continental shelf

Petroleum

Physical security

Precious metals

Precious stones

Public demonstrations

Public lands

Recreation areas

Resource shortages

Rights-of-way

State boundaries

Territories

Timber resources

Underground exploration

Waste management

Water power

Water rights

Water supply

White House facilities

Interior Department

Wilderness areas

Wildlife conservation

International Development Cooperation Agency

Disaster relief

Exports

Foreign aid

Hunger

Insurance programs

International finance

International organizations

International trade

Population growth

International Trade Commission

Copyrights

Customs

Economic data

Exports

Imports

International trade

Patents

Precious stones

Tariffs

Trade agreements

Interstate Commerce Commission

Antitrust law

Bus lines

Business regulation

Commercial law

Freight

Ground transportation

Inland waterways

Moving industry

Railroad industry

Trucking industry

Water transportation

Justice Department

Aliens

Antitrust law

Bankruptcy

Border patrol

Capital punishment

Citizenship

Civil disorders

Civil procedure

Civil rights

Commercial law

Computer security

Congressional districts

Congressional employees

Congressional power

Congressional-executive relations

Constitutional amendments

Correctional facilities

Corrupt practices

Court orders

Crime data

Crime prevention

Crime victims

Criminal procedure

Debt collection

Deportation

Diplomatic immunity

Drug traffic

Elections

Eminent domain

Justice Department
Environmental liability
Espionage
Ethnic groups
Executive orders
Executive privilege
Expatriation
Extradition
Federal charters
Federal courts
Federal judges
Foreign agents
Foreign visitors
Gambling
Government information
Government liability
Government litigation
Hate crimes
Hijacking
Identity papers
Immigration
Impeachment
Indians
Industrial security
Intelligence activities
International crime
Interstate relations
Journalistic confidentiality
Judicial administration
Judicial ethics
Judicial remedies
Juries
Juvenile delinquency
Law enforcement
Legal opinions

Lobbying
Lotteries
Members of Congress
Missing children
Money laundering
National security
Naturalization
Neutrality law
Obscenity
Obstruction of justice
Organized crime
Pardons
Parole
Police misconduct
Political asylum
Polygraphs
Pornography
Presidency
Prisoners
Privacy
Product liability
Product tampering
Proprietary data
Public demonstrations
Public lands
Refugees
Religious institutions
Salvage
Sentences
Separation of powers
Smuggling
State boundaries
Subversive activities
Territorial waters
Terrorism

Justice Department

Treason

Treaties

Trials

Violent crime

Voting

War powers

Water rights

White collar crime

Wiretapping

Witness protection

Labor Department

Aliens

Apprenticeship

Chemicals

Child labor

Construction industry

Consumer Price Index

Day care

Discrimination

Drug testing

Economic data

Explosives

Fringe benefits

Government contracts

Hazardous materials

Immigration

Indians

Indoor health

Labor markets

Labor relations

Labor standards

Marine safety

Migrant workers

Mine safety

Occupational safety

Pensions

Polygraphs

Radiation

Retirement

Toxic substances

Unemployment compensation

Unemployment rate

Veterans

Vocational rehabilitation

Wages

Welfare

Workers compensation

Legal Services Corporation

Legal services

Library of Congress

Civil-military relations

Congressional operations

Congressional organization

Congressional oversight

Congressional power

Congressional-executive
  relations

Copyrights

Federal records

Government information

Libraries

Presidency

Separation of powers

War powers

Marine Mammal Commission

Wildlife conservation

Merit Systems
Protection Board

Government employees

Legal opinions

National Aeronautics and
Space Administration

Aeronautics

Astronomy

Atmosphere

Space commercialization

Space communication

Space exploration

National and Community
Service Corporation

Volunteer services

National Archives and
Records Administration

Executive orders

Federal records

Government information

Presidency

Privacy

Public administration

National Capital
Planning Commission

District of Columbia

Historic preservation

Monuments

Public buildings

National Commission on Libraries
and Information Science

Libraries

National Credit
Union Administration

Consumer credit

Credit unions

Financial institutions

National Foundation on
the Arts and Humanities

Architecture

Arts

Government fellowships

Humanities

Museums

Nonprofit organizations

Public broadcasting

Public buildings

National Labor
Relations Board

Labor relations

National Mediation Board

Aviation industry

Labor relations

Railroad industry

National Science
Foundation

Astronomy

Atmosphere

Biotechnology

Chemicals

Computer technology

Earthquake research

Electrical standards

Energy research

National Science
Foundation

Environmental research

Geology

Global environment

Government fellowships

Industrial technology

Laboratory research

Oceanography

Offshore drilling

Plastics

Polar regions

Social sciences

Technological risk

Undersea exploration

Weather

National Transportation
Safety Board

Aviation safety

Environmental liability

Hazardous materials

Highway safety

Marine safety

Mass transit

Passenger ships

Pipelines

Railroad safety

Nuclear Regulatory
Commission

Nuclear facilities

Nuclear safety

Nuclear waste

Public utilities

Radiation

Occupational Safety and
Health Review Commission

Occupational safety

Office of Personnel
Management

Drug testing

Fringe benefits

Government employees

Health insurance

Holidays

Labor relations

Pensions

Polygraphs

Public administration

Retirement

Survivor benefits

Veterans

Wages

Office of Technology
Assessment

Biotechnology

Chemicals

Computer technology

Copyrights

Drug safety

Drug testing

Energy production

Energy research

Environmental research

Genetics

Health care

Industrial pollution

Industrial technology

Laboratory research

Office of Technology
Assessment

Marine resources

Military research

Mineral resources

National security

Nuclear energy

Nuclear waste

Oceanography

Polygraphs

Privacy

Radiation

Space exploration

Strategic stockpiles

Technological risk

Telecommunications

Underground exploration

Undersea exploration

Waste management

Weapons

Weather

Panama Canal Commission

Panama Canal

Peace Corps

Volunteer services

Pennsylvania Avenue
Development Corporation

District of Columbia

Historic preservation

Pension Benefit
Guaranty Corporation

Pensions

Postal Rate Commission

Postal Service

Postal Service

Charitable organizations

Correspondence courses

Lotteries

Nonprofit organizations

Obscenity

Philately

Physical security

Pornography

Postal Service

White collar crime

Securities and
Exchange Commission

Accounting

Advertising

Bankruptcy

Business investment

Economic data

Financial institutions

Government securities

International finance

Negotiable instruments

Securities industry

White collar crime

Security and Cooperation
in Europe Commission

Human rights

Selective Service System

Selective Service

Small Business Administration

Business assistance

Business investment

Business regulation

Disaster relief

Economic data

Exports

Franchises

Government contracts

Industrial technology

Insurance programs

International trade

Rural areas

Small business

Veterans

Smithsonian Institution

Aeronautics

Animals

Arts

Environmental research

Ethnic groups

Geology

Government fellowships

Historic preservation

Horticulture

Humanities

Indians

Insects

Museums

Plants

Precious stones

Space exploration

Social Security Administration

Aged

Disability benefits

Family services

Handicapped

Homelessness

Retirement

Social Security

Survivor benefits

Trust funds

Visual disorders

Welfare

Special Counsel's Office

Government employees

State Department

Airspace

Arms control

Arms exports

Citizens abroad

Citizenship

Copyrights

Diplomatic immunity

Diplomatic recognition

Diplomatic service

Drug traffic

Environmental research

Expatriation

Exports

Extradition

Foreign aid

State Department

Foreign investments

Foreign sovereign immunity

Foreign visitors

Global environment

Human rights

Immigration

Imports

Intelligence activities

International agreements

International arbitration

International boundaries

International communication

International crime

International finance

International law

International organizations

International trade

International transportation

International travel

International waters

Legal opinions

Marine resources

Maritime industry

Martial law

Military assistance

Mineral resources

Multinational corporations

National security

Neutrality law

North Atlantic Treaty
   Organization (NATO)

Nuclear proliferation

Ocean policy

Panama Canal

Patents

Polar regions

Political asylum

Population growth

Refugees

Repatriation

Salvage

Seal of the U.S.

Space exploration

Strategic stockpiles

Technology transfer

Telecommunications

Territories

Terrorism

Trade agreements

Trade deficits

Trademarks

Treaties

Undersea exploration

Warfare

Tennessee Valley
Authority

Dams

Electric power

Flood control

Forestry

Irrigation

Land management

Public utilities

Recreation areas

Water power

Water supply

Wildlife conservation

Transportation Department

Air pollution

Transportation Department

Airports

Atmosphere

Automobile industry

Aviation industry

Aviation safety

Billboards

Bridges

Business assistance

Civil defense

Drug traffic

Freight

Ground transportation

Harbors

Hazardous materials

Highway construction

Highway safety

Hijacking

Inland waterways

International trade

International transportation

International waters

Marine safety

Maritime industry

Mass transit

Mobile homes

Ocean policy

Oil spills

Passenger ships

Pipelines

Railroad industry

Railroad safety

Rescue services

Rights-of-way

Salvage

Service academies

Smuggling

Space commercialization

Territorial waters

Time zones

Tunnels

Water transportation

Treasury Department

Accounting

Advertising

Alcoholic beverages

Arson

Bank regulation

Border patrol

Budget administration

Budget deficits

Budget formulation

Business investment

Charitable organizations

Child support

Consumer credit

Counterfeiting

Credit programs

Currency

Customs

Day care

Debt collection

Debt management

Drug traffic

Eminent domain

Explosives

Exports

Federal charters

Federal paperwork

Treasury Department

Financial institutions

Firearms

Foreign aid

Foreign currency

Foreign investments

Foreign property

Foreign taxes

Fringe benefits

Funding gaps

Government borrowing

Government securities

Government spending

Identity papers

Imports

Individual retirement accounts

Interest rates

International communication

International finance

International organizations

International trade

Law enforcement

Lobbying

Local governments

Money laundering

Money supply

Multinational corporations

Neutrality law

Nonprofit organizations

Numismatics

Pensions

Philately

Physical security

Precious metals

Presidency

Product labeling

Public debt

Real estate industry

Religious institutions

Resource shortages

Retirement

Revenue sharing

Securities industry

Smuggling

State governments

Tariffs

Taxation

Technology transfer

Tobacco industry

Trade deficits

Trust funds

White collar crime

United States
Information Agency

Expositions

Foreign visitors

International communication

International travel

United States
Institute of Peace

International arbitration

Veterans Affairs Department

Correspondence courses

Disability benefits

Health care

Hospital regulation

Veterans Affairs Department

Insurance programs

Mortgage loans

Pensions

Rehabilitation services

Survivor benefits

Veterans

Vocational education

Vocational rehabilitation

Volunteer services

CONGRESSIONAL COMMITTEES BY PARENT AGENCY

	HOUSE	SENATE	FUNDING
ACTION (5,18)	EE	LA	LAB
Administrative Conference of the United States (10, 14)	GR JU	GA JU	TRE
Advisory Commission on Inter-governmental Relations (10)	GR	GA	TRE
Agriculture Department (1, 4, 9, 11, 12, 13, 16, 17, 18)	AG (JEC)	AG	AGR INT
Architect of the Capitol (10)	HO	RU	LEG
Arms Control and Disarmament Agency (13, 15)	IR	FR	COM
Civil Rights Commission (14)	JU	JU	COM
Commerce Department (2, 3, 4, 8, 9, 10, 13, 16, 17)	CO SC (JEC)	CO EP	COM
Commodity Futures Trading Commission (1, 2)	AG	AG	AGR
Congressional Budget Office (9, 10)	BU	BU	LEG
Consumer Product Safety Commission (2, 5, 11)	CO	CO	VA
Defense Department (4, 7, 13, 15, 16, 17)	IN NS	AR INT	DEF MC
Education Department (3, 5, 18)	EE	LA	LAB
Energy Department (2, 7, 8, 15, 16, 17)	CO, RE, SC (JEC)	EN	ENER INT
Environmental Protection Agency (8, 11, 16)	CO	EP	VA
Equal Employment Opportunity Commission (6, 14)	EE	LA	COM
Executive Office of the President (8, 9, 10, 13, 14, 15, 17)	BA, CO, GR, JU, NS, SC (JEC)	AR, DA, CO, EP, GA, JU	COM DEF TRE VA
Export-Import Bank of the United States (2, 13)	BA (JEC)	BA	FO
Farm Credit Administration (1, 9)	AG	AG	AGR
Federal Communications Commission (2, 3, 13, 14)	CO	CO	COM
Federal Deposit Insurance Corporation (9)	BA	BA	*
Federal Election Commission (10, 14)	HO	RU	TRE

*This is a self-sustaining agency and does not receive any appropriated funds

	HOUSE		SENATE	FUNDING
Federal Emergency Management Agency (4, 8, 12, 15)	TR		EP	VA
Federal Housing Finance Board (9)	BA		BA	VA
Federal Labor Relations Authority (6, 10)	EE GR		GA LA	TRE
Federal Maritime Commission (2, 13, 19)	TR		CO	COM
Federal Mediation and Conciliation Service (6)	EE		LA	LAB
Federal Mine Safety and Health Review Commission (6, 11)	EE		LA	LAB
Federal Reserve System (2, 9, 10, 13)	BA	(JEC)	BA	*
Federal Trade Commission (2, 3, 9, 14)	CO		CO	COM
Fine Arts Commission (5, 10)	EE		LA	INT
General Accounting Office (9, 10)	GR		GA	LEG
General Services Administration (10)	GR		GA	TRE
Government Ethics Office (10)	GR		GA	TRE
Government Printing Office (5, 10)	HO	(JCP)	RU	LEG
Health and Human Services Department (11, 12, 17, 18)	CO, EE, WM		AGI, FI, LA	AGR LAB
Housing and Urban Development Department (9, 12, 18, 20)	BA	(JEC)	BA	VA
Interior Department (7, 8, 16, 17)	RE		EN, EP, IN	ENER INT
International Development Cooperation Agency (2, 9, 13)	IR		FR	FO
International Trade Commission (2, 13)	WM	(JEC)	FI	COM
Interstate Commerce Commission (2, 19)	CO		CO	TRA
Justice Department (2, 3, 10, 13, 14)	JU		JU	COM
Labor Department (6, 11, 12, 18)	EE	(JEC)	LA	LAB
Legal Services Corporation (14)	JU		LA	COM
Library of Congress (5, 10)	HO		RU	LEG
Marine Mammal Commission (8, 16)	RE		EP	COM
Merit Systems Protection Board (10)	GR		GA	TRE
National Aeronautics and Space Administration (17, 19)	SC		CO	VA

*This is a self-sustaining agency and does not receive any appropriated funds

	HOUSE	SENATE	FUNDING
National and Community Service Corporation (5, 18)	EE	LA	VA
National Archives and Records Administration (3, 10)	GR	GA	TRE
National Capital Planning Commission (10, 20)	GR	GA	INT
National Commission on Libraries and Information Science (5)	EE	LA	LAB
National Credit Union Administration (9)	BA	BA	VA
National Foundation on the Arts and Humanities (3, 5)	EE	LA	INT
National Labor Relations Board (6)	EE	LA	LAB
National Mediation Board (6)	EE	LA	LAB
National Science Foundation (5, 17)	SC	CO	VA
National Transportation Safety Board (11, 19)	TR	CO	TRA
Nuclear Regulatory Commission (7, 11)	CO	EP	ENER
Occupational Safety and Health Review Commission (6, 11)	EE	LA	LAB
Office of Personnel Management (6, 10, 12)	GR	GA	TRE
Office of Technology Assessment (17)	SC	CO	LEG
Panama Canal Commission (2, 13, 15)	NS	AR, CO	TRA
Peace Corps (13)	IR	FR	FO
Pennsylvania Avenue Development Corporation (10, 20)	TR	EP	INT
Pension Benefit Guaranty Corporation (6, 9, 12)	EE	LA	*
Postal Rate Commission (3, 10)	GR	GA	TRE
Postal Service (3, 10)	GR	GA	TRE
Securities and Exchange Commission (2, 9)	BA CO (JEC)	BA	COM
Security and Cooperation in Europe Commission (13)	IR	FR	COM
Selective Service System (15)	NS	AR	VA
Small Business Administration (2, 4, 20)	SB (JEC)	SB	COM
Smithsonian Institution (5, 16, 17)	HO	RU	INT
Social Security Administration (9, 12, 18)	BU, CO, WM	BU, FI, LA	LAB

*This is a self-sustaining agency and does not receive any
appropriated funds

	HOUSE	SENATE	FUNDING
Special Counsel's Office (10)	GR	GA	TRE
State Department (2, 3, 10, 13, 14, 15, 19)	IR	FR	COM FO
Tennessee Valley Authority (4, 7, 16)	TR	EN EP	ENER
Transportation Department (2, 4, 8, 11, 13, 19, 20)	CO TR	CO EP	COM TRA
Treasury Department (2, 9, 10, 12, 13, 14)	BA, CO, IR, GR, JU, WM (JEC)	BA, CO, FI, FR, GA, JU	TRE
United States Information Agency (3, 13)	IR	FR	COM
United States Institute of Peace (5, 13)	EE	FR LA	LAB
Veterans Affairs Department (5, 6, 9, 11, 12, 18)	VA	VA	VA

Part 4

Congressional Committees

SPECIFIC SUBJECT CATEGORIES BY CONGRESSIONAL COMMITTEE

House Agriculture

Agricultural credit

Agricultural development

Agricultural markets

Agricultural production

Agricultural research

Agricultural subsidies

Agricultural surpluses

Animals

Birds

Child nutrition

Commodity markets

Consumer education

Crops

Dairy industry

Disaster relief

Economic data

Exports

Fibers

Fire control

Flood control

Food distribution

Food inspection

Food stamps

Foreclosure

Forestry

Fruits

Grains

Grazing lands

Herbicides

Home economics

Horticulture

Hunger

Insects

International trade

Irrigation

Land management

Livestock

Meat

Nutrition

Pesticides

Plants

Poultry

Rural areas

Soil conservation

Sugar

Timber resources

Tobacco industry

Water supply

Wildlife conservation

House Appropriations

Budget administration

Credit programs

District of Columbia

Executive branch operations

Funding gaps

Government spending

Impoundments

House Banking and Financial Services

Advertising

Bank deposits

Bank regulation

Building standards

Business assistance

Business investment

House Banking and Financial Services

Commercial credit

Commercial law

Construction industry

Consumer credit

Credit programs

Credit unions

Crime victims

Currency

Depressed areas

Discrimination

Economic controls

Economic data

Exports

Federal charters

Financial institutions

Foreclosure

Foreign currency

Foreign investments

Government contracts

Government securities

Gross Domestic Product

Historic preservation

Homelessness

Homesteading

Housing industry

Housing management

Individual retirement accounts

Insurance industry

Insurance programs

Interest rates

International finance

International organizations

International trade

Land management

Land sales

Money laundering

Money supply

Mortgage loans

Negotiable instruments

Numismatics

Nursing homes

Precious metals

Public housing

Real estate industry

Securities industry

Slum clearance

White collar crime

House Budget

Budget deficits

Budget formulation

Credit programs

Economic data

Government spending

Public debt

Social Security

Taxation

Trust funds

House Commerce

Abortion

Accounting

Acid rain

Acquired immune deficiency syndrome (AIDS)

Advertising

Aged

Air pollution

Alcoholic beverages

Alcoholism

House Commerce

Allergies

Antitrust law

Arthritis

Atmosphere

Automobile industry

Aviation industry

Bacteriology

Biotechnology

Blood

Broadcasting

Burn injuries

Bus lines

Business investment

Business regulation

Cancer

Chemicals

Child health

Coal

Commercial law

Communicable diseases

Consumer credit

Consumer education

Consumer protection

Correspondence courses

Cosmetics industry

Debt collection

Dentistry

Discrimination

Drug abuse

Drug safety

Drug testing

Eating disorders

Electric power

Energy conservation

Energy consumption

Energy data

Energy prices

Energy production

Energy research

Energy storage

Environmental liability

Environmental protection

Epidemiology

Ethnic groups

Exports

Expositions

Family planning

Foreign investments

Franchises

Genetics

Global environment

Government publications

Ground transportation

Handicapped

Hazardous materials

Health care

Health data

Health insurance

Health maintenance
   organizations

Hearing disorders

Heart disease

Herbicides

Highway safety

Homelessness

Hospital facilities

Hospital regulation

Hydroelectric power

Immunization

Imports

House Commerce

Indoor health

Industrial pollution

Industrial technology

Infant mortality

Insurance industry

International communication

International trade

International transportation

International travel

Interstate relations

Learning disabilities

Mapping

Medical devices

Medical laboratories

Medical research

Mental health

Mining industry

Mobile homes

Moving industry

Natural gas

Negotiable instruments

Neurological diseases

Noise pollution

Nuclear energy

Nuclear facilities

Nuclear safety

Nuclear waste

Nursing homes

Nutrition

Offshore drilling

Oil spills

Organ transplants

Orthopedics

Pesticides

Petroleum

Physical education

Plastics

Population growth

Precious stones

Prenatal care

Preventive medicine

Product labeling

Product liability

Product safety

Product tampering

Proprietary data

Public broadcasting

Public utilities

Radiation

Radon

Recording industry

Rehabilitation services

Resource shortages

Respiratory diseases

Securities industry

Skin diseases

Smoking

Social Security

Space communication

Sports

Survivor benefits

Technology transfer

Telecommunications

Time zones

Tobacco industry

Tourism

Toxic substances

Trauma

Trucking industry

House Commerce

Venereal disease

Visual disorders

Vocational rehabilitation

Waste management

Water pollution

Water power

Water supply

Water transportation

House Economic and
Educational Opportunities

Adult education

Aged

Aliens

Apprenticeship

Architecture

Arts

Bilingual education

Chemicals

Child abuse

Child labor

Child nutrition

Child support

Compensatory education

Construction industry

Consumer Price Index

Correspondence courses

Day care

Debt collection

Disability benefits

Discrimination

Economic data

Education data

Education research

Elementary education

Explosives

Family services

Food distribution

Fringe benefits

Government contracts

Government fellowships

Handicapped

Higher education

Home economics

Homelessness

Humanities

Hunger

Juvenile delinquency

Laobr markets

Labor relations

Labor standards

Learning disabilities

Libraries

Literacy

Migrant workers

Mine safety

Missing children

Museums

Nutrition

Occupatinal safety

Pensions

Polygraphs

Preschool education

Private schools

Public schools

Radiation

Refugees

Rehabilitation services

Retirement

Secondary education

House Economic and Educational Opportunities

Sports

Student loans

Unemployment rate

Vocational education

Vocational rehabilitation

Volunteer services

Wages

Welfare

Workers compensation

House Government Reform and Oversight

Accounting

Administrative law

Advisory committees

Architecture

Budget administration

Budget formulation

Census

Computer security

Computer technology

Congressional operations

Congressional organization

Congressional oversight

Congressional-executive relations

Consumer education

District of Columbia

Drug testing

Eminent domain

Executive branch operations

Executive branch organization

Executive orders

Executive privilege

Federal charters

Federal paperwork

Federal property

Federal records

Fringe benefits

Government contracts

Government corporations

Government employees

Government ethics

Government information

Government procurement

Government spending

Health insurance

Holidays

Homelessness

Identity papers

Inspectors General

Interagency relations

Intergovernmental relations

Labor relations

Legal opinions

Local governments

Lotteries

Medal of Freedom

Occupational safety

Pensions

Philately

Physical security

Polygraphs

Postal Service

Presidency

Privacy

Public administration

Retirement

Revenue sharing

Separation of powers

House Government
Reform and Oversight

State governments

Survivor benefits

Wages

House Oversight

Arts

Capitol facilities

Congressional employees

Congressional operations

Elections

Federal records

Government publications

Historic preservation

Humanities

Libraries

Lobbying

Members of Congress

Monuments

Museums

Physical security

Presidency

House Intelligence

Intelligence activities

House International Relations

Airspace

Arms control

Arms exports

Border patrol

Citizens abroad

Civil-military relations

Congressional-executive relations

Customs

Diplomatic immunity

Diplomatic recognition

Diplomatic service

Disaster relief

Drug traffic

Espionage

Expatriation

Exports

Expositions

Extradition

Foreign aid

Foreign investments

Foreign property

Foreign visitors

Human rights

Hunger

Imports

Intelligence activities

International agreements

International arbitration

International boundaries

International claims

International communication

International crime

International finance

International law

International organizations

International trade

International transportation

International travel

International waters

Military assistance

Multinational corporations

National security

Neutrality law

House _International_ _Relations_

North Atlantic Treaty
  Organization (NATO)

Nuclear proliferation

Nuclear testing

Ocean policy

Polar regions

Political asylum

Population growth

Refugees

Repatriation

Salvage

Smuggling

Terrorism

Treaties

Volunteer services

War powers

Warfare

House _Judiciary_

Abortion

Administrative law

Alcoholic beverages

Aliens

Antitrust law

Arson

Bankruptcy

Border patrol

Capital punishment

Citizenship

Civil disorders

Civil procedure

Civil rights

Civil-military relations

Commercial law

Computer security

Congressional districts

Congressional power

Congressional-executive
  relations

Constitutional amendments

Copyrights

Correctional facilities

Corrupt practices

Counterfeiting

Court orders

Crime data

Crime prevention

Crime victims

Criminal procedure

Debt collection

Deportation

Diplomatic immunity

Discrimination

Drug traffic

Elections

Espionage

Ethnic groups

Executive orders

Executive privilege

Expatriation

Explosives

Extradition

Federal charters

Federal courts

Federal judges

Firearms

Flag of the U.S.

Foreign agents

Foreign sovereign immunity

Foreign visitors

Gambling

House Judiciary

Government ethics

Government information

Government liability

Government litigation

Hate crimes

Hijacking

Holidays

Immigration

Impeachment

Intelligence activities

International crime

Interstate relations

Journalistic confidentiality

Judicial administration

Judicial ethics

Judicial remedies

Juries

Juvenile delinquency

Law enforcement

Legal opinions

Legal services

Lobbying

Lotteries

Missing children

Naturalization

Obscenity

Obstruction of justice

Organized crime

Pardons

Parole

Patents

Police misconduct

Political asylum

Polygraphs

Pornography

Presidency

Prisoners

Privacy

Product liability

Product tampering

Public demonstrations

Recording industry

Refugees

Religious institutions

Seal of the U.S.

Sentences

Separation of powers

Smuggling

State boundaries

Subversive activities

Terrorism

Territories

Trademarks

Treason

Trials

Violent crime

Voting

White collar crime

Wiretapping

Witness protection

House National Security

Airspace

Armed forces

Arms control

Arms exports

Civil defense

Government contracts

Government procurement

House National Security

Industrial security

Intelligence activities

Mapping

Marine Corps

Martial law

Medal of Honor

Military assistance

Military installations

Military law

Military operations

Military personnel

Military research

National Guard

National security

Nuclear energy

Nuclear proliferation

Nuclear testing

Panama Canal

Selective Service

Service academies

Space communication

Strategic stockpiles

Telecommunications

Wages

Warfare

Weapons

House Resources

Animals

Birds

Coal

Coastal zone management

Dams

District of Columbia

Earthquake research

Electric power

Endangered species

Energy production

Energy research

Environmental protection

Environmental research

Flood control

Forestry

Geology

Grazing lands

Historic preservation

Hydroelectric power

Indians

Inland waterways

Irrigation

Land management

Mapping

Marine resources

Mineral leases

Mineral resources

Mining industry

Monuments

Nuclear energy

Nuclear facilities

Nuclear safety

Nuclear waste

Oceanography

Offshore drilling

Outer continental shelf

Petroleum

Pipelines

Public lands

Public utilities

Radiation

House Resources

Recreation areas

Resource shortages

Rights-of-way

Territorial waters

Territories

Timber resources

Underground exploration

Undersea exploration

Water power

Water rights

Water supply

White House facilities

Wilderness areas

Wildlife conservation

House Rules

Budget formulation

Congressional-executive relations

Congressional operations

Congressional organization

Congressional oversight

Impoundments

House Science

Aeronautics

Agricultural research

Air pollution

Astronomy

Atmosphere

Aviation industry

Biotechnology

Building standards

Chemicals

Coal

Computer security

Computer technology

Earthquake research

Electric power

Electrical standards

Endangered species

Energy research

Environmental liability

Environmental research

Explosives

Fire control

Genetics

Global environment

Government publications

Ground transportation

Handicapped

Herbicides

Highway safety

Industrial technology

Laboratory research

Marine resources

Medical research

Mineral resources

Natural gas

Noise pollution

Nuclear energy

Nuclear waste

Nutrition

Ocean policy

Oceanography

Offshore drilling

Patents

Petroleum

Plastics

Polar regions

House Science

Privacy

Radiation

Social sciences

Space commercialization

Space communication

Space exploration

Strategic stockpiles

Technological risk

Technology transfer

Telecommunications

Toxic substances

Underground exploration

Waste management

Water pollution

Water supply

Weather

Weights and measures

House Small Business

Antitrust law

Business assistance

Business investment

Business regulation

Commercial law

Disaster relief

Exports

Franchises

Government contracts

Industrial technology

Insurance programs

International trade

Occupational safety

Rural areas

Small business

House Standards of
Official Conduct

Corrupt practices

Members of Congress

House Transportation
and Infrastructure

Airports

Automobile industry

Aviation industry

Aviation safety

Billboards

Bridges

Business assistance

Capitol facilities

Dams

Depressed areas

Disaster relief

District of Columbia

Electric power

Eminent domain

Environmental liability

Flood control

Freight

Ground transportation

Harbors

Hazardous materials

Highway construction

Highway safety

Inland waterways

International transportation

Marine safety

Maritime industry

Mass transit

Mobile homes

Ocean policy

House Transportation and Infrastructure

Oil spills

Passenger ships

Pipelines

Public buildings

Public utilities

Railroad industry

Railroad safety

Rescue services

Salvage

Territorial waters

Trucking industry

Tunnels

Waste management

Water pollution

Water power

Water supply

Water transportation

White House facilities

House Veterans Affairs

Disability benefits

Health care

Hospital regulation

Insurance programs

Mortgage loans

Pensions

Rehabilitation services

Survivor benefits

Trust funds

Veterans

Vocational education

Vocational rehabilitation

House Ways and Means

Accounting

Aged

Budget administration

Budget deficits

Business investment

Charitable organizations

Child support

Customs

Day care

Debt collection

Debt management

Federal paperwork

Foreign investments

Foreign taxes

Fringe benefits

Funding gaps

Government borrowing

Government securities

Handicapped

Health insurance

Health maintenance
    organizations

Homelessness

Imports

Individual retirement
    accounts

Interest rates

International finance

International trade

Lobbying

Multinational corporations

Nonprofit organizations

Nursing homes

Precious stones

House Ways and Means

Public debt

Real estate industry

Religious institutions

Retirement

Revenue sharing

Social Security

Tariffs

Taxation

Tobacco industry

Trade agreements

Trade deficits

Trust funds

Unemployment compensation

Welfare

Senate Aging

Aged

Senate Agriculture,
Nutrition, and Forestry

Jurisdiction is identical to
House Agriculture Committee

Senate Appropriations

Jurisdiction is identical to
House Appropriations Committee

Senate Armed Services

Jurisdiction is identical to
House National Security Committee with the following
exception: excludes Industrial
security

Senate Banking, Housing,
and Urban Affairs

Jurisdiction is identical to
House Banking and Financial
Services Committee with the
following exceptions: includes

Accounting and Mass transit;
excludes Historic preservation

Senate Budget

Jurisdiction is identical to
House Budget Committee

Senate Commerce, Science,
and Transportation

Advertising

Aeronautics

Airports

Alcoholic beverages

Antitrust law

Astronomy

Atmosphere

Automobile industry

Aviation industry

Aviation safety

Biotechnology

Broadcasting

Building standards

Bus lines

Business investment

Business regulation

Chemicals

Coastal zone management

Commercial law

Computer technology

Consumer credit

Consumer education

Consumer protection

Correspondence courses

Cosmetics industry

Debt collection

Discrimination

Senate Commerce, Science, and Transportation

Drug testing

Earthquake research

Electrical standards

Endangered species

Environmental research

Ethnic groups

Explosives

Exports

Expositions

Fire control

Franchises

Freight

Genetics

Geology

Global environment

Government publications

Ground transportation

Harbors

Hazardous materials

Herbicides

Highway safety

Imports

Industrial technology

Inland waterways

International communication

International trade

International transportation

International travel

International waters

Interstate relations

Laboratory research

Mapping

Marine resources

Marine safety

Maritime industry

Mobile homes

Moving industry

Natural gas

Noise pollution

Ocean policy

Oceanography

Offshore drilling

Oil spills

Outer continental shelf

Panama Canal

Passenger ships

Patents

Pipelines

Plastics

Polar regions

Precious stones

Privacy

Product labeling

Product liability

Product safety

Proprietary data

Public broadcasting

Radiation

Railroad industry

Railroad safety

Recording industry

Rescue services

Resource shortages

Salvage

Service academies

Space commercialization

Space communication

Space exploration

Sports

Senate Commerce, Science, and Transportation

Technological risk

Technology transfer

Telecommunications

Territorial waters

Time zones

Tobacco industry

Tourism

Trucking industry

Underground exploration

Undersea exploration

Water pollution

Water transportation

Weather

Weights and measures

Senate Energy and Natural Resources

Coal

Coastal zone management

Dams

Electric power

Energy conservation

Energy consumption

Energy data

Energy prices

Energy production

Energy research

Energy storage

Environmental protection

Flood control

Forestry

Geology

Grazing lands

Harbors

Historic preservation

Hydroelectric power

Industrial pollution

Inland waterways

Irrigation

Land management

Mineral leases

Mineral resources

Mining industry

Monuments

Natural gas

Nuclear energy

Nuclear safety

Nuclear waste

Offshore drilling

Outer continental shelf

Petroleum

Pipelines

Public lands

Public utilities

Recreation areas

Resource shortages

Rights-of-way

Territories

Timber resources

Underground exploration

Undersea exploration

Water power

Water rights

Water supply

Wilderness areas

Wildlife conservation

Senate Environment
and Public Works

Acid rain

Air pollution

Animals

Atmosphere

Automobile industry

Aviation industry

Billboards

Birds

Bridges

Business assistance

Capitol facilities

Coal

Dams

Depressed areas

Disaster relief

District of Columbia

Earthquake research

Electric power

Eminent domain

Endangered species

Environmental liability

Environmental protection

Environmental research

Flood control

Global environment

Ground transportation

Harbors

Hazardous materials

Herbicides

Highway construction

Highway safety

Industrial pollution

Inland waterways

International transportation

Mapping

Marine resources

Noise pollution

Nuclear energy

Nuclear facilities

Nuclear safety

Nuclear waste

Ocean policy

Oil spills

Public buildings

Public utilities

Radiation

Radon

Respiratory diseases

Toxic substances

Tunnels

Waste management

Water pollution

Water power

Water supply

Water transportation

White House facilities

Wildlife conservation

Senate Ethics

Jurisdiction is identical to
House Standards of Official
Conduct Committee

Senate Finance

Jurisdiction is identical to
House Ways and Means Committee

Senate Foreign Relations

Jurisdiction is identical to
House International Relations
Committee with the following
exception: includes Foreign
agents

Senate Governmental Affairs

Jurisdiction is identical to
House Government Reform and
Oversight Committee with the
following exceptions: includes

Arson

Charitable organizations

Health maintenance organizations

Lobbying

Nuclear energy

Nuclear facilities

Nuclear proliferation

Nuclear waste

Organized crime

Public buildings

Senate Indian Affairs

Indians

Senate Intelligence

Jurisdiction is identical to
House Intelligence Committee

Senate Judiciary

Jurisdiction is identical to
House Judiciary Committee with
the following exceptions:
includes Industrial security
and Insurance industry;
excludes Foreign agents,
Legal services, and Lobbying

Senate Labor and Human Resources

Abortion

Acquired immune deficiency
  syndrome (AIDS)

Adult education

Aged

Alcoholism

Aliens

Allergies

Apprenticeship

Architecture

Arthritis

Arts

Bacteriology

Bilingual education

Biotechnology

Blood

Burn injuries

Cancer

Chemicals

Child abuse

Child health

Child labor

Child support

Communicable diseases

Compensatory education

Construction industry

Consumer Price Index

Correspondence courses

Cosmetics industry

Day care

Dentistry

Disability benefits

Discrimination

Drug abuse

Drug safety

Drug testing

Eating disorders

Economic data

Education data

Education research

Elementary education

Epidemiology

Explosives

Family planning

<u>Senate Labor and</u>
<u>Human Resources</u>

Family services

Food inspection

Genetics

Government contracts

Government fellowships

Health care

Health data

Health insurance

Health maintenance
  organizations

Hearing disorders

Heart disease

Higher education

Home economics

Homelessness

Hospital facilities

Hospital regulation

Humanities

Hunger

Immunization

Indoor health

Infant mortality

Juvenile delinquency

Labor markets

Labor relations

Labor standards

Learning disabilities

Legal services

Libraries

Literacy

Medical devices

Medical laboratories

Medical research

Mental health

Migrant workers

Mine safety

Missing children

Museums

Neurological diseases

Nursing homes

Nutrition

Occupational safety

Organ transplants

Orthopedics

Pensions

Pesticides

Physical education

Polygraphs

Population growth

Prenatal care

Preschool education

Preventive medicine

Private schools

Product tampering

Public schools

Radiation

Refugees

Rehabilitation services

Respiratory diseases

Retirement

Secondary education

Skin diseases

Smoking

Social sciences

Social Security

Sports

Student loans

Survivor benefits

Toxic substances

Senate Labor and
Human Resources

Trauma

Unemployment rate

Venereal disease

Visual disorders

Vocational education

Vocational rehabilitation

Volunteer services

Wages

Welfare

Workers compensation

Senate Rules and
Administration

Jurisdiction is identical to
House Oversight Committee
with the following exception:
excludes Impoundments

Senate Small Business

Jurisdiction is identical to
House Small Business Committee

Senate Veterans Affairs

Jurisdiction is identical to
House Veterans Affairs Committee

Joint Economic

Business regulation

Commercial credit

Commercial law

Consumer Price Index

Economic data

Financial institutions

Foreign investments

Gross Domestic Product

Housing industry

Industrial technology

Interest rates

International trade

Labor markets

Labor relations

Multinational corporations

Public debt

Real estate industry

Small business

Tariffs

Taxation

Trade deficits

Unemployment rate

Wages

Joint Printing

Government publications

PARENT AGENCIES AND APPROPRIATIONS SUBCOMMITTEES
BY LEGISLATIVE COMMITTEE

House Committees	PARENTS	SENATE	FUNDING
Agriculture (1, 4, 9, 11, 12, 13, 16, 17, 18)	AGR CFTC FCA	AG (JEC)	AGR
Banking and Financial Services (2, 9, 10, 12, 13, 18, 20)	EOP EXIM FDIC FHFB FRB HUD NCUA SEC TRE	BA (JEC)	COM TRE VA
Budget (9, 10)	CBO	BU	LEG
Commerce (2, 3, 4, 7, 8, 9, 11, 13, 14, 15, 16, 17, 18, 19)	COM CPSC ENR EOP EPA FCC FTC HHS ICC SEC SSA TRA TRE	DA CO EN EP LA (JEC)	COM ENER INT LAB TRA TRE VA
Economic and Educational Opportunities (3, 5, 6, 11, 12, 17, 18)	ACTION EDU EEOC FAC FLRA FMCS FMSH HHS LAB NCLIS NCSC NFAH NLRB NMB OSHR PBGC USIP	LA (JEC)	INT LAB
Government Reform and Oversight (3, 6, 9, 10, 12, 14, 20)	ACIR ACUS EOP FLRA GAO GEO GSA MSPB NARA NCPC OPM PRC PS SCO TRE	GA	DC LEG TRE

House Committees	PARENTS	SENATE		FUNDING
House Oversight (5, 10, 14)	ARC FEC GPO LC SI	RU	(JCP)	INT LEG
Intelligence (13, 15)	DEF EOP JUS STA TRE	INT		DEF
International Relations (2, 3, 9, 10, 13, 14, 15)	ACDA IDCA PCO SCEC STA TRE USIA	FR		COM FO
Judiciary (2, 3, 10, 14)	ACUS CRC JUS LSC TRE	JU		COM TRE
National Security (4, 7, 13, 15, 16, 17)	DEF EOP PCC SSS	AR		DEF MC
Resources (2, 5, 7, 8, 10, 11, 16, 17, 20)	INT MMC NRC PADC	EN EP IN		ENER INT
Rules (10)		RU		LEG
Science (2, 3, 7, 8, 17, 20)	COM ENR EOP NASA NSF OTA	CO EN		COM ENER INT VA
Small Business (2, 4, 20)	SBA	SB	(JEC)	COM
Standards of Official Conduct (10)	JUS	ET		LEG
Transportation and Infrastructure (4, 7, 8, 16, 17, 19, 20)	FEMA FMC NTSB TRA TVA	CO EP GA		TRA TRE
Veterans Affairs (5, 6, 9, 11, 12, 18)	VA	VA		VA
Ways and Means (2, 9, 10, 11, 12, 13, 18)	ITC SSA TRE	FI	(JEC)	COM LAB TRE

Senate Committees	PARENTS	HOUSE	FUNDING
Aging (5, 6, 11, 12, 18)	EDU	EE	LAB
	HHS	WM	VA
	HUD		
	LAB		

Agriculture, Nutrition, and Forestry (Identical to House
Agriculture Committee)

Armed Services (Identical to House National Security Committee)

Banking, Housing, and Urban Affairs (Identical to House Banking and
Financial Services Committee)

Budget (Identical to House Budget Committee)

	PARENTS	HOUSE	FUNDING
Commerce, Science, and	COM	CO	COM
Transportation (2, 3, 4,	CPSC	SC	TRA
8, 9, 11, 13, 14, 17, 19)	EOP	TR	TRE
	FCC		VA
	FMC	(JEC)	
	FTC		
	ICC		
	NASA		
	NSF		
	NTSB		
	OTA		
	PCC		
	TRA		
	TRE		
Energy and Natural Resources	ENR	CO	ENER
(2, 7, 8, 15, 16, 17)	INT	RE	INT
	TVA	SC	(JEC)
Environment and Public Works	COM	CO	COM
(2, 4, 7, 8, 10, 11,	EPA	SC	ENER
16, 17, 19, 20)	FEMA	TR	INT
	INT		TRA
	MMC		VA
	NRC		
	PADC		
	TRA		
	TVA		

Ethics (Identical to House Standards of Official Conduct Committee)

Finance (Identical to House Ways and Means Committee)

Foreign Relations (Identical to House International Relations
Committee with addition of one Parent Agency:
USIP)

Governmental Affairs (Identical to House Government Reform and
Oversight Committee)

Indian Affairs (16, 18)	EDU	RE	INT
	HHS		LAB
	HUD		
	INT		
	LAB		

Intelligence (Identical to House Intelligence Committee)

Judiciary (Identical to House Judiciary Committee)

Senate Committees	PARENTS	HOUSE	FUNDING
Labor and Human Resources	ACTION	CO	COM
(3, 5, 6, 11, 12, 17, 18)	EDU	EE	INT
	EEOC		LAB
	FAC	(JEC)	
	FLRA		
	FMCS		
	FMSH		
	HHS		
	LAB		
	LSC		
	NCLIS		
	NCSC		
	NFAH		
	NLRB		
	NMB		
	OSHR		
	PBGC		
	SSA		
	USIP		

Rules and Administration (Identical to House Oversight Committee)

Small Business (Identical to House Small Business Committee)

Veterans Affairs (Identical to House Veterans Affairs Committee)

Joint Committees	PARENTS	HOUSE	SENATE	FUNDING
Economic (1, 2,	AGR	AG	AG	AGR
6, 7, 9, 12)	COM	BA	BA	COM
	ENR	CO	CO	ENER
	EOP	EE	EN	FO
	EXIM	SB	FI	LAB
	FRB	TR	LA	TRE
	HUD	WM	SB	VA
	ITC			
	LAB			
	SBA			
	SEC			
	TRE			
Printing (10)	GPO	HO	RU	LEG

Part 5

Appropriations Subcommittees

SPECIFIC SUBJECT CATEGORIES BY APPROPRIATIONS SUBCOMMITTEE

Agriculture, Rural Development,
and Related Agencies

Agricultural credit

Agricultural development

Agricultural markets

Agricultural production

Agricultural research

Agricultural subsidies

Agricultural surpluses

Animals

Birds

Child nutrition

Commodity markets

Crops

Dairy industry

Disaster relief

Fibers

Flood control

Food distribution

Food inspection

Food stamps

Foreclosure

Fruits

Grains

Herbicides

Home economics

Horticulture

Hunger

Insects

Irrigation

Livestock

Meat

Nutrition

Pesticides

Plants

Poultry

Rural areas

Soil conservation

Sugar

Tobacco industry

Departments of Commerce,
Justice, State, and the
Judiciary and Related
Agencies

Accounting

Administrative law

Advertising

Air pollution

Airspace

Aliens

Antitrust law

Arms control

Atmosphere

Automobile industry

Bankruptcy

Biotechnology

Border patrol

Broadcasting

Building standards

Business assistance

Business investment

Business regulation

Capital punishment

Census

Chemicals

Citizens abroad

Citizenship

Civil disorders

Departments of Commerce, Justice, State, and the Judiciary and Related Agencies

Civil procedure

Civil rights

Coastal zone management

Commercial credit

Commercial law

Computer security

Computer technology

Congressional districts

Constitutional amendments

Consumer credit

Consumer education

Consumer protection

Copyrights

Correctional facilities

Correspondence courses

Corrupt practices

Court orders

Crime data

Crime prevention

Crime victims

Criminal procedure

Customs

Debt collection

Deportation

Depressed areas

Diplomatic immunity

Diplomatic recognition

Diplomatic service

Discrimination

Drug traffic

Economic data

Electrical standards

Eminent domain

Endangered species

Environmental research

Espionage

Ethnic groups

Executive privilege

Expatriation

Exports

Expositions

Extradition

Federal charters

Federal courts

Federal judges

Fire control

Firearms

Foreign agents

Foreign aid

Foreign investments

Foreign sovereign immunity

Foreign visitors

Franchises

Freight

Gambling

Global environment

Government corporations

Government information

Government liability

Government litigation

Gross Domestic Product

Harbors

Hijacking

Human rights

Identity papers

Immigration

Impeachment

Imports

Departments of Commerce,
Justice, State, and the
Judiciary and Related
Agencies

Industrial security

Industrial technology

Inland waterways

Insurance industry

International agreements

International boundaries

International claims

International communication

International crime

International finance

International law

International trade

International transportation

International travel

International waters

Interstate relations

Journalistic confidentiality

Judicial administration

Judicial ethics

Judicial remedies

Juries

Juvenile delinquency

Laboratory research

Law enforcement

Legal opinions

Legal services

Lobbying

Local governments

Lotteries

Mapping

Marine resources

Maritime industry

Mineral leases

Money laundering

Multinational corporations

National security

Naturalization

Negotiable instruments

Neutrality law

North Atlantic Treaty
    Organization (NATO)

Nuclear proliferation

Obscenity

Obstruction of justice

Ocean policy

Oceanography

Organized crime

Panama Canal

Pardons

Parole

Passenger ships

Patents

Plastics

Polar regions

Police misconduct

Political asylum

Polygraphs

Pornography

Precious stones

Presidency

Prisoners

Privacy

Product labeling

Product liability

Product safety

Product tampering

Proprietary data

Public broadcasting

Public demonstrations

Departments of Commerce, Justice, State, and the Judiciary and Related Agencies

Recording industry

Refugees

Religious institutions

Repatriation

Resource shortages

Salvage

Seal of the U.S.

Securities industry

Sentences

Separation of powers

Small business

Smuggling

Space communication

Sports

State boundaries

Strategic stockpiles

Subversive activities

Tariffs

Technology transfer

Telecommunications

Territorial waters

Territories

Terrorism

Tourism

Trade agreements

Trade deficits

Trademarks

Treason

Treaties

Trials

Undersea exploration

Violent crime

Voting

War powers

Warfare

Water pollution

Water transportation

Weather

Weights and measures

White collar crime

Wildlife conservation

Wiretapping

Witness protection

Defense Department

Armed forces

Arms control

Arms exports

Civil defense

Espionage

Government contracts

Government procurement

Industrial security

Intelligence activities

Mapping

Marine Corps

Martial law

Medal of Honor

Military assistance

Military law

Military operations

Military personnel

Military research

National Guard

National security

North Atlantic Treaty
  Organization (NATO)

Defense Department
Nuclear proliferation
Nuclear testing
Ocean policy
Oceanography
Service academies
Strategic stockpiles
Technology transfer
Warfare
Weapons

District of Columbia
District of Columbia

Energy and Water Development
Coal
Dams
Electric power
Energy conservation
Energy consumption
Energy prices
Energy production
Energy research
Energy storage
Flood control
Hydroelectric power
Irrigation
Nuclear energy
Nuclear facilities
Nuclear safety
Nuclear testing
Nuclear waste
Offshore drilling
Petroleum
Pipelines

Proprietary data
Public utilities
Radiation
Resource shortages
Underground exploration
Water power
Water rights
Water supply
Weapons

Foreign Operations, Export
Financing, and Related
Programs
Arms exports
Exports
Foreign aid
Human rights
International finance
International organizations
International trade
Military assistance
Population growth
Volunteer services

Interior Department
and Related Agencies
Animals
Architecture
Arts
Birds
Coal
Earthquake research
Endangered species
Energy consumption
Energy data
Energy prices

Interior Department
and Related Agencies

Energy production

Energy research

Environmental protection

Fire control

Forestry

Geology

Grazing lands

Historic preservation

Humanities

Indians

Land management

Mapping

Marine resources

Mine safety

Mineral leases

Mineral resources

Mining industry

Monuments

Museums

Natural gas

Offshore drilling

Outer continental shelf

Petroleum

Precious metals

Precious stones

Public buildings

Public demonstrations

Public lands

Recreation areas

Rights-of-way

Territories

Timber resources

Underground exploration

Water supply

White House facilities

Wilderness areas

Wildlife conservation

Departments of Labor, Health
and Human Services, and Education, and Related Agencies

Abortion

Acquired immune deficiency
  syndrome (AIDS)

Adult education

Aged

Alcoholism

Aliens

Allergies

Apprenticeship

Arthritis

Bacteriology

Bilingual education

Biotechnology

Blood

Burn injuries

Cancer

Child abuse

Child health

Child labor

Child support

Communicable diseases

Compensatory education

Consumer Price Index

Correspondence courses

Day care

Dentistry

Disability benefits

Discrimination

Departments of Labor, Health
and Human Services, and Education, and Related Agencies

Drug abuse

Drug testing

Eating disorders

Economic data

Education data

Education research

Elementary education

Epidemiology

Family planning

Family services

Fringe benefits

Genetics

Government contracts

Government fellowships

Handicapped

Health care

Health data

Health insurance

Health maintenance organizations

Hearing disorders

Heart disease

Higher education

Home economics

Homelessness

Hospital facilities

Hospital regulation

Immunization

Indians

Indoor health

Infant mortality

Juvenile delinquency

Labor markets

Labor relations

Labor standards

Learning disabilities

Libraries

Literacy

Medical devices

Medical laboratories

Medical research

Mental health

Migrant workers

Mine safety

Missing children

Neurological diseases

Nursing homes

Occupational safety

Organ transplants

Orthopedics

Pensions

Physical education

Polygraphs

Population growth

Prenatal care

Preschool education

Preventive medicine

Private schools

Public schools

Radiation

Refugees

Rehabilitation services

Respiratory diseases

Retirement

Secondary education

Skin diseases

Smoking

Social Security

Sports

Departments of Labor, Health
and Human Services, and Education, and Related Agencies

Student loans

Survivor benefits

Toxic substances

Trauma

Trust funds

Unemployment compensation

Unemployment rate

Venereal disease

Veterans

Visual disorders

Vocational education

Vocational rehabilitation

Volunteer services

Wages

Welfare

Workers compensation

Legislative Branch

Capitol facilities

Congressional employees

Congressional operations

Congressional organization

Congressional oversight

Congressional power

Congressional-executive relations

Constitutional amendments

Copyrights

Elections

Government publications

Impeachment

Libraries

Members of Congress

Separation of powers

War powers

Military Construction

Military installations

Transportation Department
and Related Agencies

Airports

Automobile industry

Aviation industry

Aviation safety

Billboards

Bridges

Bus lines

Business assistance

Environmental liability

Freight

Ground transportation

Harbors

Hazardous materials

Highway construction

Highway safety

Hijacking

Inland waterways

International transportation

Marine safety

Maritime industry

Mass transit

Moving industry

Oil spills

Panama Canal

Passenger ships

Pipelines

Railroad industry

Railroad safety

Transportation Department
and Related Agencies

Rescue services

Rights-of-way

Service academies

Smuggling

Space commercialization

Territorial waters

Time zones

Trucking industry

Tunnels

Water transportation

Treasury, Postal Service,
and General Government

Accounting

Administrative law

Advisory committees

Alcoholic beverages

Arson

Bank regulation

Border patrol

Budget administration

Budget deficits

Budget formulation

Business investment

Charitable organizations

Civil-military relations

Computer security

Congressional-executive relations

Counterfeiting

Credit programs

Currency

Customs

Debt collection

Debt management

Drug testing

Drug traffic

Economic controls

Elections

Executive branch operations

Executive branch organization

Executive orders

Executive privilege

Explosives

Federal charters

Federal paperwork

Federal property

Federal records

Financial institutions

Firearms

Foreign currency

Foreign property

Foreign taxes

Fringe benefits

Funding gaps

Government borrowing

Government employees

Government ethics

Government information

Government procurement

Government securities

Government spending

Health insurance

Holidays

Identity papers

Impoundments

Individual retirement
  accounts

Inspectors General

Interagency relations

<u>Treasury</u>, <u>Postal Service</u>,
<u>and</u> <u>General</u> <u>Government</u>

Interest rates

Intergovernmental relations

International trade

Labor relations

Law enforcement

Legal opinions

Lobbying

Local governments

Lotteries

Medal of Freedom

Money laundering

Money supply

Multinational corporations

Negotiable instruments

Nonprofit organizations

Numismatics

Pensions

Philately

Physical security

Polygraphs

Postal Service

Precious metals

Presidency

Privacy

Public administration

Public buildings

Public debt

Resource shortages

Retirement

Revenue sharing

Securities industry

State governments

Strategic stockpiles

Survivor benefits

Tariffs

Taxation

Tobacco industry

Trade agreements

Trust funds

Wages

White collar crime

White House facilities

<u>Departments</u> <u>of</u> <u>Veterans</u>
<u>Affairs</u>, <u>Housing</u> <u>and</u>
<u>Urban</u> <u>Development</u>, <u>and</u>
<u>Independent</u> <u>Agencies</u>

Acid rain

Aeronautics

Air pollution

Arson

Astronomy

Atmosphere

Bank deposits

Bank regulation

Building standards

Chemicals

Civil defense

Computer technology

Construction industry

Consumer education

Consumer protection

Credit unions

Depressed areas

Disability benefits

Disaster relief

Electrical standards

Energy storage

Environmental liability

Environmental protection

Environmental research

Departments of Veterans
Affairs, Housing and
Urban Development, and
Independent Agencies

Financial institutions

Foreclosure

Global environment

Government corporations

Hazardous materials

Health care

Herbicides

Homelessness

Homesteading

Hospital regulation

Housing industry

Housing management

Industrial pollution

Industrial technology

Insurance programs

Interest rates

Land sales

Mining industry

Mobile homes

Mortgage loans

Noise pollution

Oil spills

Pensions

Pesticides

Plastics

Polar regions

Product labeling

Product liability

Product safety

Public housing

Radiation

Radon

Real estate industry

Rehabilitation services

Selective Service

Slum clearance

Social sciences

Space commercialization

Space communication

Space exploration

Survivor benefits

Technological risk

Toxic substances

Trust funds

Undersea exploration

Veterans

Vocational education

Vocational rehabilitation

Waste management

Water pollution

Weather

PARENT AGENCIES AND LEGISLATIVE COMMITTEES
BY APPROPRIATIONS SUBCOMMITTEE

Subcommittees	PARENTS	HOUSE		SENATE
Agriculture, Rural Development, and Related Agencies (1, 2, 4, 9, 11, 12, 16, 17, 18)	AGR (except FS) CFTC FCA FDA (HHS)	AG (JEC)		AG
Departments of Commerce, Justice, State, and the Judiciary and Related Agencies (2, 3, 4, 8, 9, 10, 13, 14, 15, 16, 17, 19)	ACDA COM CRC EEOC FCC FMC FTC ITC JUS LSC MA (TRA) MMC SBA SCEC SEC STA (except INM, IOA, RPB) TRO (EOP) USIA	BA CO EE IR JU SB WM (JEC)		BA CO FI FR JU LA SB
Defense Department (7, 13, 16, 16, 17)	CIA (EOP) DEF	IN NS		AR INT
District of Columbia (10, 20)		GR		GA
Energy and Water Development (2, 7, 8, 11, 15, 16, 17)	ACE (DEF) ENR (except EIA, ERA, FEO) NRC RB (INT) TVA	CO RE TR (JEC)		EN EP
Foreign Operations, Export Financing, and Related Programs (2, 9, 13, 15)	EXIM IDCA INM (STA) IOA (STA) PCO RPB (STA)	IR NS		AR FR
Interior Department and Related Agencies (1, 3, 5, 7, 8, 10, 16, 17, 20)	EIA (ENR) ERA (ENR) FAC FEO (ENR) FS (AGR) INT (except RB) NCPC NFAH PADC SI	AG CO EE GR HO RE TR		AG EN EP GA IN LA RU

Subcommittees	PARENTS	HOUSE	SENATE
Departments of Labor, Health and Human Services, and Education, and Related Agencies (3, 5, 6, 11, 12, 17, 18)	ACTION EDU FMCS FMSH HHS (except FDA) LAB NCLIS NLRB NMB OSHR SSA USIP	CO EE WM (JEC)	AGI FI LA
Legislative Branch (5, 9, 10, 14)	ARC CBO GAO GPO LC OTA	BU GR HO JU RU ST (JCP)	BU ET GA JU RU
Military Construction (4, 15)	DEF	NS	AR
Transportation Department and Related Agencies (2, 4, 8, 11, 13, 19)	ICC NTSB PCC TRA (except MA)	CO TR	CO

Treasury, Postal Service, and General Government (2, 3, 6, 9, 10, 13, 14)	ACIR
	ACUS
	EOP (except CEQ,
	       CIA, STP,
	       TRO)
	FEC
	FLRA
	GEO
	GSA
	MSPB
	NARA
	OPM
	PRC
	PS
	SCO
	TRE
		GR
		HO
		JU
		WM
		(JEC)
			FI
			GA
			JU
			RU

Departments of Veterans Affairs, Housing and Urban Development, and Independent Agencies (2, 4, 5, 8, 9, 11, 12, 16, 17, 18, 19, 20)	CEQ (EOP) CPSC EPA FEMA FHFB HUD NASA NCSC NCUA NSF SSS STP (EOP) VA	BA CO GR SC VA (JEC)	BA CO EP GA VA

Index
(Agency/Committee Abbreviations)

Parent Agencies

ACDA Arms Control and Disarmament Agency: 7, 41, 86, 87, 92, 113, 139, 140, 156

ACIR Advisory Commission on Intergovernmental Relations: 32, 36, 52, 85, 91, 113, 139, 157

ACTION 35, 57, 84, 87, 91, 113, 139, 142, 157

ACUS Administrative Conference of the United States: 5, 46, 85, 86, 91, 113, 140, 157

AGR Agriculture Department: 6, 9, 11, 14, 16, 18-25, 27-31, 33-36, 41, 43, 45-48, 50, 52, 53, 55, 58, 59, 84-87, 91, 92, 113, 139, 142, 156

ARC Architect of the Capitol: 11, 85, 92, 113, 140, 157

CBO Congressional Budget Office: 10, 16, 19, 27, 28, 43, 47, 54, 56, 85, 93, 113, 139, 157

CFTC Commodity Futures Trading Commission: 13, 45, 53, 84, 93, 113, 139, 156

COM Commerce Department: 6, 8 13, 16, 17, 19-25, 27, 30-34, 36, 38-42, 44-49, 51-56, 58, 59, 84-87, 92, 93, 113, 139-142, 156

CPSC Consumer Product Safety Commission: 14, 22, 28, 44, 46, 55, 84, 86, 93, 113, 139, 141, 157

CRC Civil Rights Commission: 12, 57, 86, 92, 113, 140, 156

DEF Defense Department: 6, 7, 8, 12, 16, 19, 22, 24, 26, 27, 31, 32, 33, 36-41, 44, 46, 51-54, 56, 57, 58, 84-87, 93, 94, 113, 140, 156, 157

EDU Education Department: 5, 8, 13, 15, 18, 20, 26-30, 34, 35, 37, 45, 46, 47, 49, 50, 52, 53, 56, 57, 84, 87, 94, 113, 139, 141, 142, 157

EEOC Equal Employment Opportunity Commission: 7, 18, 57, 85, 86, 95, 113, 139, 142, 156

ENR Energy Department: 7, 12, 20, 21, 22, 30, 31, 40, 41, 43, 46-49, 53, 56, 58, 84, 85, 87, 94, 95, 113, 139-142, 156

EOP Executive Office of the President: 5, 9, 10, 12, 13, 14, 16-27, 30-33, 36-42, 45-48, 52, 54-58, 84-87, 95, 96, 97, 113, 139-142, 156, 157

EPA Environmental Protection Agency: 5-8, 11, 21, 28, 30, 31, 38, 40, 41, 43, 48, 54, 55, 58, 85, 86, 87, 95, 113, 139, 141, 157

EXIM Export-Import Bank of the United States: 10, 22, 32, 84, 86, 97, 113, 139, 142, 156

FAC Fine Arts Commission: 7, 39, 47, 84, 85, 98, 114, 139, 142, 156

FCA Farm Credit Administration: 6, 84, 85, 97, 113, 139, 156

FCC Federal Communications Commission: 5, 7, 9, 10, 32, 41, 47, 48, 52, 54, 84, 86, 97, 113, 139, 141, 156

FDIC Federal Deposit Insurance Corporation: 8, 14, 23, 38, 40, 85, 97, 113, 139

Agency Subunits

AA   Aging Administration (HHS): 6

ACE   Army Corps of Engineers (DEF): 12, 16, 24, 31

ACS   Agricultural Cooperative Service (AGR): 6

AF   Air Force Department (DEF): 6, 7, 51

AG   Attorney General (JUS): 14, 22, 23, 30, 34, 45, 51, 57

AID   Agency for International Development (IDCA): 18, 24, 30, 44

AMS   Agricultural Marketing Service (AGR): 6, 16, 23, 25, 27, 35,
        36, 45, 55

ANT   Antitrust Division (JUS): 7

APHIS   Animal and Plant Health Inspection Service (AGR): 6, 9, 20,
        29, 31, 35, 43, 45

APO   Acquisition Policy Office (GSA): 27

ARMY   Army Department (DEF): 7, 51

ARPA   Advanced Research Projects Agency (DEF): 38

ARS   Agricultural Research Service (AGR): 6, 14, 16, 28, 31, 43

ASCS   Agricultural Stabilization and Conservation Service (AGR):
        6, 16, 23, 27, 52, 53, 55

ATF   Alcohol, Tobacco and Firearms Bureau (TRE): 5, 6, 7, 22,
        23, 34, 46, 55

BE   Bilingual Education and Minority Language Affairs Office
        (EDU): 8

BGA   Block Grant Assistance Office (HUD): 17

CAB   Consular Affairs Bureau (STA): 12, 22, 25, 30, 32, 33

CAS   Civil Aviation Security Office (TRA): 28

CB   Census Bureau (COM): 11, 13, 19, 21, 36, 44, 49, 52

CC   Comptroller of the Currency (TRE): 8, 13, 14, 16, 23, 39

CCC   Commodity Credit Corporation (AGR): 6

CCCI   Command, Control, Communications and Intelligence Office
        (DEF): 19, 32, 37, 54

CDC   Centers for Disease Control and Prevention (HHS): 5, 13,
        21, 30, 45, 56

CEA   Council of Economic Advisers (EOP): 10, 19, 27, 54

CEP   Compensatory Education Programs Office (EDU): 13, 34, 35, 37

CEQ   Council on Environmental Quality (EOP): 5, 21

CG   Coast Guard (TRA): 9, 12, 19, 27, 31, 33, 36, 41, 42, 44,
        49, 50, 51, 54, 58

CHB   Childrens' Bureau (HHS): 17, 45

CIA   Central Intelligence Agency (EOP): 21, 32, 36, 52

Agency Subunits

EAB   Economic Analysis Bureau (COM): 10, 19, 27 55

EBA   Economic and Business Affairs Bureau (STA): 7, 15, 22, 24, 30, 32, 33, 36, 39, 40, 42, 53, 55

ECA   Educational and Cultural Affairs Bureau (STA): 25, 32

EDA   Economic Development Administration (COM): 10, 17

EEO   Environment and Energy Office (HUD): 20, 21, 34, 58

EIA   Energy Information Administration (ENR): 20

EOIR   Executive Office for Immigration Review (JUS): 30

EPB   Engraving and Printing Bureau (TRE): 15, 16, 27, 43

EPO   Economic Policy Office (TRE): 10, 19

ERA   Economic Regulatory Administration (ENR): 12, 20, 40, 43

ERI   Educational Research and Improvement Office (EDU): 20, 35

ERO   Energy Research Office (ENR): 21

ERS   Economic Research Service (AGR): 19

ES   Extension Service (AGR): 6, 29, 50

ESA   Employment Standards Administration (LAB): 11, 26, 34, 37, 44, 57

ESE   Elementary and Secondary Education Office (EDU): 20, 45, 46, 47, 50

ESH   Environment, Safety and Health Office (ENR): 21, 40, 41, 48

ETA   Employment and Training Administration (LAB): 6, 7, 30, 34, 37, 56, 57, 58

ETO   Emergency Transportation Office (TRA): 12, 49

EUR   European and Canadian Affairs Bureau (STA): 40

EUSA   Executive Office for U.S. Attorneys (JUS): 15, 16, 17, 25, 27, 34, 41, 42, 56, 57, 59

EUST   Executive Office for U.S. Trustees (JUS): 8

EXP   Export Administration Bureau (COM): 22, 54

FAA   Federal Aviation Administration (TRA): 6, 8, 25, 28, 51

FACO   Foreign Assets Control Office (TRE): 24

FAHA   Farmers Home Administration (AGR): 6, 18, 24, 50

FAO   Family Assistance Office (HHS): 17, 58

FAS   Foreign Agricultural Service (AGR): 6, 22, 24, 30, 33

FBI   Federal Bureau of Investigation (JUS): 12, 16, 19, 21, 25, 27, 28, 32, 34, 38, 42, 44, 46, 53, 54, 55, 57, 58

FCIC   Federal Crop Insurance Corporation (AGR): 16

FCSC   Foreign Claims Settlement Commission (JUS): 32

Agency Subunits

Agency Subunits

IPO   Information and Privacy Office (JUS): 26, 46

IPR   Intelligence Policy and Review Office (JUS): 32, 40

IRB   Intelligence and Research Bureau (STA): 32

IRMS   Information Resources Management Service (GSA): 13, 26

IRS   Internal Revenue Service (TRE): 5, 10, 11, 17, 20, 23, 25, 30, 34, 36, 38, 39, 40, 43, 48, 49, 54, 55, 58

ISA   International Security Affairs Office (DEF): 7, 37, 41

ISO   Information Security Oversight Office (GSA): 26

ISP   International Security Policy Office (DEF): 7, 40, 41, 57

ITA   International Trade Administration (COM): 22, 24, 33, 39, 40, 45, 49, 55

JAB   Justice Assistance Bureau (JUS): 15, 16, 19, 45, 57

JAG   Judge Advocate General (DEF: AF/ARMY/NAVY): 37

JCS   Joint Chiefs of Staff (DEF): 36, 37, 40

JJDP   Juvenile Justice and Delinquency Prevention Office (JUS): 34, 38

JMD   Justice Management Division (JUS): 33

JPO   Justice Programs Office (JUS): 16

JSB   Justice Statistics Bureau (JUS): 16, 27, 58

LAO   Legal Adviser's Office (STA): 6, 12, 18, 22, 25, 32, 33, 35, 40, 50, 55

LCO   Legal Counsel's Office (JUS): 14, 18, 22, 23, 27, 33, 35, 55

LEI   Law Enforcement and Intelligence Affairs Office (STA): 22, 32

LMB   Land Management Bureau (INT): 12, 25, 27, 34, 38, 47, 48, 49, 55, 58, 59

LMR   Labor-Management Relations Bureau (LAB): 19, 34

LMS   Labor-Management Standards Office (LAB): 34

LNR   Land and Natural Resources Division (JUS): 20, 21, 30, 47, 54, 58

LPD   Library Programs Division (EDU): 35

LSB   Labor Statistics Bureau (LAB): 14, 19, 28, 56, 57

LSO   Liaison Services Office (JUS): 33, 52

MA   Maritime Administration (TRA): 10, 27, 31, 33, 36, 41, 51, 58

MAO   Monetary Affairs Office (TRE): 38

MB   Mines Bureau (INT): 38, 45, 49, 56

MBDA   Minority Business Development Agency (COM): 51

Agency Subunits

OSHA   Occupational Safety and Health Administration (LAB):
       7, 11, 14, 28, 30, 36, 40, 41, 48, 55

PAO   Pardon Attorney's Office (JUS): 42

PB   Prisons Bureau (JUS): 15, 45

PBS   Public Buildings Service (GSA): 7, 29, 43, 47, 58

PC   Parole Commission (JUS): 42, 45

PDB   Public Debt Bureau (TRE): 10, 17, 25, 26, 27, 32, 47

PDO   Policy Development Office (JUS): 11, 12, 16, 23, 34,
       44, 56, 59

PDR   Policy Development and Research Office (HUD): 29, 51

PE   Postsecondary Education Office (EDU): 5, 13, 26, 28,
       46, 47, 52, 53

PHO   Public Housing Office (HUD): 47

PHS   Public Health Service (HHS): 5, 22, 28, 43, 45

PIA   Pacific Island Affairs Office (STA): 54

PMA   Politico-Military Affairs Bureau (STA): 6, 7, 18, 32,
       36, 37, 40, 57

PO   Protocol Office (STA): 18

PRE   Private Education Office (EDU): 46

PSA   Packers and Stockyards Administration (AGR): 35, 36, 45

PSO   Pipeline Safety Office (TRA): 43

PTO   Patent and Trademark Office (COM): 42, 55

PWBA   Pension and Welfare Benefits Administration (LAB):
       25, 43, 49

RAW   Remedial Action and Waste Technology Office (ENR): 41

RB   Reclamation Bureau (INT): 16, 24, 30, 31, 33, 48, 58, 59

RDA   Rural Development Administration (AGR): 50

REA   Rural Electrification Administration (AGR): 6, 50

REO   Research and Engineering Office (DEF): 27, 38, 58

RPB   Refugee Programs Bureau (STA): 48, 49

RRO   Refugee Resettlement Office (HHS): 48

RSA   Rehabilitation Services Administration (EDU): 27, 49

RSO   Revenue Sharing Office (TRE): 36, 49, 52

SAO   Security Affairs Office (ENR): 31

SBD   Savings Bond Division (TRE): 27

SC   Sentencing Commission (JUS): 51

Senate Committees

About the Compiler

JERROLD ZWIRN is a reference librarian in a branch of the District of Columbia Public Library. He is the author of *Congressional Publications,* (1983), *Congressional Publications and Proceedings* (1988), and the earlier edition of this guide published by Greenwood Press in 1989.

ISBN 0-313-29765-7

90000>

EAN

9 780313 297656

HARDCOVER BAR CODE